PR...
CAMINO FORWARD

"With a spirit of honesty, humility, and vulnerability, Miguel provides personal insight into the experiences, struggles, and aspirations he faced that motivated him to support young scholars whose backgrounds mirror his. He shares the "why" and "how" he created a successful program to help students who need role models and help as they navigate school life and prepare for a career. His passion project touched and impacted our students in ways our school system had not witnessed before. Interwoven with the personal reflections of his and others, Miguel's message and lessons learned prove that there really is a Camino Forward!"

—Dr. Paul Cruz, former Superintendent,
Austin Independent School District

"Miguel Romano clearly understands the importance of creating hope in students who are growing up like many of us Hispanics. With *Camino Forward*, Miguel celebrates the successes of many Hispanics and, by highlighting their stories and lessons learned, Miguel creates opportunities for hope with these students and their families, teachers, and friends."

—Sara Martinez Tucker, former President & CEO of the
Hispanic Scholarship Fund and Undersecretary of Education,
U.S. Department of Education

CAMINO
FORWARD

INSPIRATIONAL STORIES TO
PLAN YOUR UNIQUE PATH

CAMINO
FORWARD

MIGUEL ROMANO, JR.

RIVER GROVE
BOOKS

Published by River Grove Books
Austin, TX
www.rivergrovebooks.com

Distributed by River Grove Books

Design and composition by Greenleaf Book Group
Cover design by Greenleaf Book Group

Publisher's Cataloging-in-Publication data is available.

Print ISBN: 978-1-63299-577-3

eBook ISBN: 978-1-63299-578-0

First Edition

To Madre & Papi and Mama & Pepe:
My camino forward began with your dreams and sacrifices.

To Ellie & Tomas:
Our family's story continues with your future.

CONTENTS

YOU ARE NOT ALONE

I t happens to me every year. Before I say a thing, the students look at me with suspicion, doubt, and skepticism. They're not saying it, but I know they're thinking it: *Who is he? Why is he here? How can he help me? This is going to be a waste of time . . .*

Once I stand in front of these teenage students, I'm on the clock. I have just a few minutes to grab their attention, earn their trust, and get them engaged.

So, I start by telling them who I am.

I am the first American in my family. My parents left a country under the reign of a dictatorship when there wasn't a lot of opportunity, but plenty of poverty.

Their dream was to start a life in the United States. With time, their dream became a reality. They sacrificed everything to start a family in their new homeland so their children might have a life they had only dreamed of.

But the life my parents started in the United States has not been easy. My family experienced cultural disconnect, language barriers, and financial distress. We were often uncomfortable in our surroundings because we looked, sounded, ate, and acted differently than those around us.

My parents realized there was a way to overcome these challenges. There was a solution to change things so their children would not have the same struggles. It was an EDUCATION. They viewed education as a difference maker. Education was the key for their children to have better lives than theirs. Education became a focus in my home.

I got it, too. I understood the importance of education. I was all in on education. It was the way out and up for my family and for me. Even though English was my second language when I started kindergarten, I worked hard to overcome an inherent disadvantage. With each year, my grades got better. I understood and valued how education would fit into my future. However, I still had a lot of questions. What is college? Can I get into college? What do I do with an education? What's my dream job? How do I make that happen?

Everyone in my family was in the restaurant business. If I wanted to start my own restaurant, I knew the business plan. However, my family wanted me to have an opportunity for a new career path.

Neither I, my parents, nor anyone else in my family knew how to plan for a career outside of the restaurant industry.

I didn't understand the endless career options that existed or how to achieve them. I didn't know the path to become a doctor, lawyer, teacher, corporate executive, or any other career. Why? Because I couldn't relate to the people who were already in those jobs. I didn't identify with them. They didn't look like me, talk like me, or come from a background like mine. Their lives were different. I'd never been exposed to them or didn't feel comfortable reaching out to them the way a lot of other students did.

I started to question how I should think about my future. What could I do? How would I do it? What was the road map to a career?

But as I asked myself these questions, I didn't feel that I had anyone to help me with the answers. I wished I had someone I could turn to. Someone I could relate to who had struggled with these same questions, someone who had been down this same path.

After telling the students my story, I would pause. I could see most of the students sit up, focus on me, and wonder what I would say next. Anyone who listened knew I could relate to them. They heard their story in my experiences. They felt my worries and pain.

If they are anything like me when I was their age . . .

They're struggling, can't find answers, can't think of a plan for their future, and don't know what they want to be, much less the career path to get there.

They're stressed out. Not only do they need to do well in school, but they also need to start thinking about a career.

Their parents are counting on them to have a brighter future than they had. That's why their family made sacrifices. If they do well, then they can lift up others in their family. They can build

3

a stronger foundation for their kids. They have the power and responsibility to change the trajectory of their family.

But if they don't figure out a career path, they feel they'll be letting down their family. All the hardships their family endured will be for nothing. They have the weight of their family on their shoulders. They're left with endless anxiety about their own future, as well as their family's future.

Their family members can't relate to their dilemma. Their friends are just as lost. Their teachers don't fully understand.

They feel deserted and isolated. They are frustrated they can't figure it out for themselves. They are scared they will disappoint their family. They are confused with the process. They are worried that they are failing to plan their future.

What I didn't realize then and what I want the students to know now is that there are others who have been in their shoes. In fact, some live in their community. And they're willing to share their stories. Students don't have to feel alone in their situation; instead, they can take comfort that others have been there, and they can learn from these individuals' experiences.

This truth is what motivated me to launch my passion project, "Camino Forward." It started as an idea aimed to encourage students to develop a career path by drawing inspiration from leaders in their community through a series of speaker forums. These gatherings give students the opportunity to learn from accomplished professionals who come from diverse careers. Speakers share their life stories and paths with the students to demonstrate the positive and negative experiences that impacted their journeys.

This book collects and expands on years of stories, lessons, and feelings shared between students and speakers. It captures a movement in our community, but also addresses a need that students, families, teachers, and schools are facing across our country.

This book is not about scientific theory. You won't find loads of statistics or research citations in the pages that follow. Nor am I a researcher with reams of data trying to make a case.

Quite simply, this is a book based on real lives—my own and others I know who've lived similar experiences. We want to help those who are living those lives now. Our common lessons learned come from the unique stories told.

The stories and lessons are captured in eight themes and summarized in chapters 3–10 in the book. But before we get there, the book starts off the same way we kick off a classroom session. I'll share more about me and the program in chapters 1 and 2 so the reader understands the purpose of Camino Forward. Our students have found it helpful and important to start with this background. We also conclude the book as we do the program—with a call to action.

If you are looking to plan your future (or help someone with theirs), the stories, lessons, and themes from Camino Forward can help. If the book is anything like our classroom sessions with the students, you will dream and hope. You will learn and plan. You will laugh and cry. You will be inspired and motivated.

You will be ready to move your (or someone else's) path forward.

CHAPTER 1

WHO AM I?

Camino Forward was meant to be about our speakers telling their stories to students. My goal was to bring accomplished and passionate speakers to the students to share their experiences and journeys while giving students access to community leaders they could relate to.

During the first year, I invited more than a dozen speakers to visit with middle school and high school students in our underserved communities. I interviewed the speakers, and the students asked them tough questions as well. The exchange was rich, educational, and emotional. In my mind, it was a perfect match of speakers and students that would ultimately spark students to think about their education and careers with a renewed sense of creativity, urgency, and excitement.

I viewed my role in this endeavor as limited and low-key. I was just the facilitator, the person who could bring these similar yet distant worlds together. I lived in both realities; I could relate to the students, and I knew our speakers. I thought my service was to make a connection and get out of the way so real impact could take place between speakers and students.

Turns out, not only did the students want to know about the speakers, but they also expected something more: They wanted to know more about me. Every year, when we started our sessions, I was peppered with questions. The questions ranged from where I was from to where I was going, and everything in between. Simple and short answers did not suffice. They were seeking details about my path.

I was trying to understand why so many questions were directed at me. With time, I think I understood why. The students were trying to figure me out. In order for them to value this program, they needed to know me. I needed to be credible to them. I had to relate to them to earn their trust. If there was any chance of them buying into Camino Forward, I had to sell myself. That's why I had to share my story as well.

I always questioned why anyone would be interested in my story. I didn't think there was anything special about it. Through Camino Forward, I've come to learn that students wanted to hear my story because it was relatable. They could understand and connect with my experiences. They were interested in my story for the same reason I was interested in theirs. I just had to do the same thing I was asking them and our speakers to do—open up and share.

I had to get comfortable quickly with sharing my ups and downs, wins and losses, and pivotal junctures in my life as teachable moments with the students. Whether I liked it or not, my personal experiences became part of the program. I couldn't sit on the sidelines and just listen to others. The choice was made for me. I had to be an active participant. My life became an open book to them.

Throughout the following chapters, you'll be learning about me—perhaps more than you want to know! My sharing of experiences is meant to highlight and reinforce the themes and learnings of the program. If I felt I owed it to the students to build a relationship of trust and credibility, I certainly also owe it to you, the reader of this book.

My path has not been perfect. I recognize that I have flaws and have made mistakes. I also recognize that I've been blessed. Throughout my journey, I've been fortunate to be surrounded by good people, to have received wise advice, and to have found myself in the right situations.

It's not been easy, and I've not always been lucky. Struggles and hardships have been constant, but so have resiliency and hard work. To understand my path, it's best for me to explain the four pillars of my life that form the foundation of the stories I'll share throughout *Camino Forward*: **family**, **education and career**, **identity**, and **purpose**.

Family

A friend and mentor of mine says that when he first meets folks and wants to learn about them, he asks them to tell him about their grandparents first, then their parents, and then themselves.

He says by the time he's heard about their parents, he's learned what has shaped the person, positively or negatively.

I asked him what his impression of me was, based on his theory. He thoughtfully replied that my family's story is one to be proud of and inspired by.

Considering how important family is to me, that compliment means the world to me. I also agree with the idea that you can learn a lot about someone by learning about their family. We're shaped by those closest to us and those who came before us. The lives our grandparents and parents lived impact the lives we inherit. We shape our own lives, but much is prescribed by the decisions made by our ancestors. Fortunately for me, my grandparents and parents made some key decisions that benefited my starting point in life.

My father, Miguel Romano, Sr., was born in Motril, Spain, a small town just outside of the larger city of Granada. My mother, Carmen Reyes Romano, was born in Cádiz, Spain, a small port town on the southwestern coast of Spain. Dreams of freedom and stability led them to a new land. At the age of 18, with no formal education and a backpack, my father left Spain for Toronto, Canada. At the same time, my mom, her siblings, and their parents left Spain and moved to Toronto as well.

They met because my father started working with my grandfather, my mom's dad, in the hotel and restaurant business. There were not many Spaniards in Toronto then. My grandfather would invite the ones he knew over to the house on Sundays for a traditional paella dinner. That's how my parents met and later married.

My dad's dream was always to live in the United States of America. One day, his friend called him from Sarasota, Florida. He said he had found him a job in a hotel and asked if he was willing to relocate. My dad said yes and immediately made the move to Sarasota. Despite some early challenges and struggles, he stuck to his dream, and my mom later joined him. He worked at that hotel, saved his money, and ultimately started his own restaurant business. Sarasota is where my parents planted roots to start their American Dream. It's also where they started a family with two boys—me and my younger brother, Jose.

In time, I found myself moving to Washington, D.C. That's where I met Katie Cook and found out that when you meet and marry a Texan, you end up in Texas. While we enjoyed our time in the nation's capital, we knew that for the next phase of our lives, we wanted to move south. Katie was kind enough to let me think my home state of Florida was on the radar for about thirty minutes; then all signs pointed to her favorite city: Austin, Texas. We moved to Austin and were blessed to start a family with our son, Miguel Thomas ("Tomas"), and daughter, Elizabeth Carmen ("Ellie").

Considering our history and migration pattern, my family has been separated by thousands of miles of water and land. But that has not limited our love for one another. We've always been close across generations and as we welcome new additions to the family. We're loving, fun, passionate, hardworking, good cooks, and loud. Actually, really loud . . . and really passionate—a dangerous combination when it comes to family dinners. Conversations are held at high decibels, even when we don't try. One time when a friend was visiting my home, my mom yelled at me from the kitchen (in Spanish). My friend, thinking we were in trouble, asked what she said. I explained that she just wanted to know if we were hungry and wanted a snack.

I'll refer regularly to my family throughout this book. I could probably write a full book or start a telenovela series on my family alone. If I'm going to share my life experiences, my family is going to be a central part of the stories and takeaways. I thought a short tutorial on this cast of notable characters in our family telenovela would be helpful as background and before I confuse you with too many names:

My mom: She has the most nicknames in my family, although she doesn't like all of them. Growing up, she was "Mommy" to us. With age, my brother and I transitioned to calling her "Madre." But the name she enjoys most now is the one my children call her: "Abueli." She starts and ends her day thinking about her family.

My father: I share the same name as him. He was "Miguel," and I was "Miguelito" or "Junior" to our family and friends. He preferred my brother and I call him "Papi" (although we spelled it "Poppy") over "Father" or "Dad". With time, my brother and I made him comfortable with the nickname "Pops." My kids never met him, but they know the stories of "Abuelo Miguel."

My brother: Jose and I are separated by five years. Like any brothers, we had our fair share of fights. But we were bound together by common history and similar circumstances, as well as a strong drive to create paths for our futures.

Mama and Pepe: My mom's parents were the matriarch and patriarch of our family. They were a constant presence in my life. They visited Florida, and we would take trips to Toronto.

They were stern, but there wasn't anything they wouldn't do for their family.

Katie: My wife of more than a decade married into a family of endless stories and drama. My family loved her from day one—and advised me early on to never let her go.

Tomas and Ellie: My son and daughter, who have allowed me to see our family's history and future through their eyes.

My family means the world to me. The experiences they faced before I was born and throughout my lifetime have impacted my path. Many family members have influenced me. They've shaped my views, personality, heart, and mind. We have cried, laughed, celebrated, and mourned together through births, Baptisms, Communions, weddings, and deaths.

Over the last few years, I've come to appreciate that I'm not the only one who feels this way about their family. If my mentor were to meet with all the speakers and students we've engaged through Camino Forward and ask them about their grandparents and parents, I know he would find family stories like mine . . . ones to be proud of and inspired by.

Education and Career

One difference between my parents, grandparents, and me is that I had the opportunity to get an education. Considering where and how they grew up, school was not really an option for them. Finances, time, and language presented barriers for them to pursue a high school diploma, much less a college degree. But that didn't mean they didn't appreciate the value and importance of schooling. It became a hallmark of their wisdom and advice to our family's next generation. They emphasized the need for an education to pursue unlimited opportunities in life. In my house, education became a requirement, not an option.

School was not easy for me, especially early on. But with hard work, focus, and help from others, I found my way in the classroom. I actually started to like school and learning—especially subjects like math and history. I went on to be the first in my family to graduate from high school, college, and graduate school. Perhaps, in a way, I was overcompensating for generations that couldn't complete their studies. My high school diploma, college degree in business communication, and two master's degrees in finance and international business have my name on them, but they represent more than just me.

However, I was naïve to think that all I had to do was earn an education and then everything would take care of itself. I came to realize that an education is just the first step in your future. You must plan a career. There are no guarantees you'll secure a job when you finish your academics. In order to secure a job, you must have a career plan. That's where I arrived late to the game.

My education positioned me to be the first in my family to think of industries beyond the restaurant business. However, not until later in college did I start seeing the endless possibilities, exploring them, and accepting jobs within them. It was a conversation with a professor that led me to an internship in Florida's capitol. A call from the White House turned into a position on a presidential campaign. An introduction by a friend turned into a stint going around the world advocating for international commerce.

My curiosity, enthusiasm, and ambition led me on an unconventional career path, with positions that were both rewarding and humbling. I've worked on high-profile campaigns but lost elections. I've drafted bills voted on in Congress, but I also had my boss's coffee order memorized. I've traveled the globe promoting trade and commerce while also seeing the world's poorest areas. I've advised companies about their external relationships while getting caught in my organization's own internal conflict. I've advised political candidates, yet I've also seen the best and worst of politics. I've helped businesses grow while seeing others fail. I've witnessed medical miracles for patients while other families deal with heartbreak and loss.

Each experience was driven by my personal interests, passions, and relationships. It took time, focus, dedication, and advice to help me along my career decisions.

I only wish I had started my career planning earlier. I wish I had dared to think bigger and asked more questions early on and more frequently. While I'm grateful and appreciative of the education I received and the jobs I've held, I'm still left wondering and have plenty of "what-ifs." What if I had . . .

- Worked harder in high school?

- Learned an instrument?

- Gone to another college or business school?

- Picked a different focus in college?

- Made different friends?

- Joined the military?

Fortunately, I can remind myself that my path continues with more opportunities (planned or unexpected) in my future.

Sometimes I still don't know what I want to be when I grow up. But every time I hear students share their educational and career dreams, I get inspired to consider a new career idea or maybe even to go back to college for another degree . . .

Identity

I not only struggled with knowing what I wanted to be when I grew up, but I also questioned who I was and how I fit in.

I wrestled with my identity growing up in Sarasota, Florida. There weren't many people I could relate to when it came to culture, language, and family experiences. When I was young, less than 10 percent of the area I lived in was Hispanic. Sarasota was not like Tampa or Miami—cities in Florida with thriving and growing Hispanic communities. Its demographic makeup is much different from the densely Hispanic-populated cities I now see in Texas. In Sarasota, I didn't know many people outside of my family who spoke with an accent, ate arroz con pollo, listened to Flamenco, watched telenovelas, or lived the lives of immigrants.

I was mostly surrounded by a White, non-Hispanic community. I assimilated into my surroundings and connected to new people with different experiences over time through church, school, and sports. My teachers, coaches, friends, and girlfriends were non-Hispanic Whites. Eventually, I became just as comfortable in their living rooms as in mine.

My ease in these different surroundings didn't come at the expense of appreciating my roots. My family instilled a deep sense of pride in our history, language, traditions, and customs. It just meant that I found myself almost straddling two different worlds.

Throughout my life, I navigated situations in which I was the odd person out. I was regularly the only Hispanic in the room. It was also common for me to be the only one in a group of Hispanics with roots outside of Latin America. In both circumstances, I often felt different and left out. Sometimes Hispanic jokes were made in front of me with no inclination of my Hispanic origins. Other times, people spoke behind my back in Spanish without having a clue that I understood every word.

People were confused by my different skin tone, hair color, accent, and name; and had different criteria to evaluate where I fit in. They questioned my authenticity and validity in either category. Was I White enough? Was I Hispanic enough? For some, the answer was no to both.

The rejection, and even just the questioning, brought self-doubt and insecurities. I struggled to understand who I was or where my place was. Perhaps even more detrimental, I questioned if it could limit where I was going. Like when I was the only one in a middle school class to be called by my last name. The teacher said it was easier to pronounce my last name than my first name. It made me question whether I should change my name to "Mike."

For many years, I shied away from talking about or sharing my identity. Now I lean into it. I speak openly about it. The old feelings of shame and confusion have been replaced by pride and confidence. I learned, after years of tears from rejection, confusion, and frustration, that no one's perception of who you are or where you fit in should cause doubt in your abilities. Nor should they limit your path.

Unfortunately, over the years, I've seen students struggle with their identity as well. From the looks on their faces and their line of questioning, I can tell they feel that other people have already made up their minds in defining them—their past, present, and future. The students feel their path is limited because of where they come from, where they live, how they speak, or the money in their pockets. They're boxed in with set expectations of who they are and what they can be.

I also know firsthand that those students' limiting frames of mind can be expanded. I've witnessed students come to appreciate their differences, understand their value, and plan for their future. It's reminded me that discovering and embracing who we are is more powerful than denying it, hiding it, or letting anyone else define it.

Purpose

Statistically speaking, I beat the odds. Someone with my background has less of a chance to graduate from high school, earn college and graduate degrees, and find a job. The inherent obstacles associated with being a first-generation American, Hispanic, low-income, or ESL (English as a second language) student often limits individuals' upward mobility. Chances of higher education and financial security can be slim.

I fully recognize and appreciate my good fortune. In many ways, I've achieved the American Dream. But with it comes a sense of guilt. Why me? Why did I have this path while others like me don't? There should be so many more who share in the American Dream. I don't want my story to be the exception to the rule or the anomaly. I want my experience to be the standard. The expectation.

To make that happen, I understand I have to do my part.

My path was made possible due to the sacrifices my grandparents and parents made. I view my obligation as continuing to create stepping-stones for my children and to grow a generational foundation for my family to build upon. While my grandfather and father made decisions that positioned our family's future, I view my role as extending this mission of opportunity outside of our family and going beyond to help other kids I can relate to as they set out on their camino.

I needed help along my journey. Without the support, advice, and love of many, I wouldn't be where I am. It took many people to position me to pursue academic and professional aspirations. I want to do that for others.

It's taken me time, maturity, and reflection to have the outlook I have today.

I used to be *motivated by what I didn't have growing up.* Primarily, that meant an education and money. My family didn't have much of either. I was driven to obtain both so I could help my family.

Then I was *motivated by what I did have.* The birth of my son and daughter instilled in me a parental and familial commitment to provide them with a secure future.

Now I'm *motivated by what I have but others don't.* I believe in the adage and Scripture that says to whom much is given, much is expected. It's not just about me or my family. Over the years, I've developed a renewed spirit and spark to help others the same way so many hands have lifted me up.

My motivation also comes with a sense of urgency. Not only because I see the growing need, but because of my own circumstances as well. Throughout this passion project, I often think of my father. He not only serves as inspiration, but also as a reminder of time passing. He died when I was young and needed him most. I'm now not far from the age he was when he passed away. Our lives can always change, so I feel I'm on the clock to do what I can now to honor him and help others.

The challenge with *wanting* to help is discovering *how* to help. The unknown with wanting to help others is whether others want your help. When I set a course to help students years ago, I wasn't sure how to do it or how it would be received. I was humbled to see the reaction by students, teachers, school administrators, and speakers to Camino Forward, such as . . .

- The class thank-you notes
- The student who chased after the speaker and asked for her contact information to stay in touch
- The principal shaking my hand with sincere gratitude
- The speaker who asked to come back for more sessions

It confirmed that there was a need and I was on the right track. But it also highlighted that I had work to do!

Since I started Camino Forward, I've learned a lot about myself. Memories, feelings, and experiences have resurfaced. Some were painful and hard to relive. Others triggered joy and happiness.

I've become comfortable sharing these snapshots of my life. I've opened up to relative strangers about my most vulnerable moments. Many of those moments that I share in this book will be a surprise to some of my family and friends. I haven't always been great at sharing my views and emotions with others; instead, I've kept them as secrets. I was either too embarrassed or too proud to share them with even those I was closest to.

But Camino Forward has taught me that if you're going to ask students (or a reader) who they are and what they want to be, you'd better come fully prepared to share the same about yourself first. That's why I tell *Who I Am*.

CHAPTER 2

WHY CAMINO FORWARD?

W hen I first meet students, they ask, "What is Camino Forward?" I tend to shift the premise of their question and answer by explaining, "Why Camino Forward?" The "what" is the result of the "why." The "why" drives everything. I think it's critical for the students to understand the "why" behind Camino Forward . . .

- Why does it matter?

- Why are people involved?

- Why should they care?

- Why can it help them?

Those are the questions they should be asking. They're the same questions I ask myself. The answers are built on the four pillars of the program: **the need, storytelling, speakers, and students**.

Before we get into the inspirational stories and themes of our chapters, I think it would be helpful to understand the genesis of Camino Forward through these pillars.

The Need

The moment I moved to Austin, I knew I wanted to be part of and contribute to the community. I think many of us want to support efforts we can relate to. So, within the first few weeks of moving to Austin, I googled "first-generation, low-income college student." Two groups popped up. I called them both and asked how I could help.

One of the organizations was Subiendo, an initiative at The University of Texas at Austin that seeks to empower the next generation of Texas leaders and encourages them to pursue higher education and civic engagement in critical fields. Subiendo asked if I would join a panel of professionals and speak to a group of high school students from across the state who aspired to be leaders. These were talented kids already planning to go to college, so I didn't have to convince them of the need for higher education. The line of questioning from the students centered on, "What is college like?" and "What happens after college?"

One of the students specifically asked, "What was the

hardest part about college?" My answer . . . "finishing." I told them it's not just about getting to college. You have to finish. I almost didn't. I withdrew from college and almost never went back.

I had never shared that story with anyone outside of family and close friends. It unexpectedly came out, along with tears and emotion. It felt good to share. But as I left the panel, I didn't know how my experiences made the students feel. Had I shared too much? Had I scared them? Was I off message? I wondered about the effects of my comments, assuming the worst. A few weeks later, I received a package with dozens of cards from the students. I sat at the kitchen table reading, crying, and reflecting. The students had written me notes of thanks and appreciation. Perhaps the one that struck me the most was this one:

I'm dating a "Miguel," and his father too also passed away this summer due to a medical problem. He also has similar ambition as yourself and when I spoke to him, I told him of your story; it inspired him just as much as it did me.

It hit me . . . these students need and are looking for advice, direction, and help from individuals to whom they can relate—people who look like them, speak like them, and think like them. These students need to hear from individuals who have lived similar lives and can share experiences that will give them insight for planning their future. It's the same thing I was looking for when I was their age but I couldn't find.

The students I met through Subiendo were from across the state and already planning their caminos. I wondered who was doing this for our local students in Austin. Who was asking Hispanic business and community leaders to share their stories with our students? These are the same leaders I happen to now call mentors and friends, but never had access to when I was younger. I asked around our community, part of me expecting someone would point to a group that was already doing it or give me a reason it was a bad idea. Instead, it was suggested I had a unique approach and good idea worth exploring.

The need was clear; the solution was not. So, I went to work to see what I could do. I researched our city's demographics and local schools. I called principals and administrators. Some took my calls; others did not. Several of the principals and school administrators I approached with this idea looked at me with skepticism . . . perhaps rightfully so. But I was able to convince others to take a chance. They allowed me the opportunity to assist them with a clear need for their students, school, and community.

The first year I launched this effort, I worked with a high school and middle school. I invited speakers and conducted interviews in front of the students. I would prompt the conversation, and the students would jump in with questions. I took copious notes to make sure I captured the speakers' and students' interactions and words.

After the initial year, I took some time to read and reflect through my notes. I found there were consistent themes that resulted from our speakers' stories, students' questions, and their mutual interactions. We found a common curiosity and emphasis among these areas. We shaped the following years to have our speakers and gatherings focus on the importance and significance of these crucial 8 Themes:

- Remember Where You Come From

- Family Matters

- Embrace Your Differences

- Each Path Is Unique

- Education Changes Lives

- Seize Opportunities

- Create Positive Surroundings

- Ask for Help

The program has evolved in other ways. In order to keep the students engaged, I start sessions with questions (asking them what country they want to travel to most is my favorite), I hand out swag (the Camino Forward journals are a hit for notetaking), teachers give extra credit for participation (one teacher would quiz the students after class; I thought it was great, the students not so much), and we incorporate visual and audio content in the presentations for effect (biographic videos are great at capturing the students' attention).

CAMINO *FORWARD*

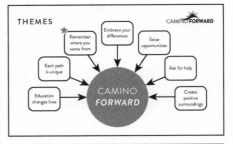

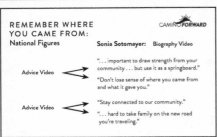

Presentation example from classroom sessions.

During the first year, I was asked what I called this project. I didn't have a name. I thought about my grandfather. He was always looking for a path—a path to make a better life for him and his family. A path forward, or as he would probably refer to it, a "Camino Forward."

Since then, Camino Forward has partnered with local schools and nonprofits to host close to 50 speakers and 50 sessions for more than 200 students. There have been more than 1,000 exchanges between our speakers and students during which stories are told, lessons are learned, and lives are impacted.

Speaking at various classroom sessions with students.

After each session and year, I still ask myself, "Is there a need and is Camino Forward helping to solve it?" When I receive a note from one of the school principals saying, "You will never know how much you are appreciated," I figure we're on the right track.

Storytelling

When I was young, I asked my relatives to tell me about our family. I loved to hear stories about their lives in Spain and their brave journeys to lands of opportunity. The places they worked (cities, hotels, and restaurants), the businesses they started (restaurants and more restaurants), the people they met (musicians, actors, politicians, executives), and even the family drama that surrounded them (arguments, fights, celebrations, parties)—I wanted to hear about it all.

I found the rich history they shared entertaining. The tales made me laugh and cry. They grounded me with humility while also inspiring me. Personal stories became the best way I absorbed information, connected with people, and understood my surroundings. They were not just history lessons, but also hints for the future. The stories were part of my education.

As we prepare our young students for successful career paths, I believe there is nothing more important than their academic education. It is the essential foundation that drives their ability to succeed. However, it's not the sole driver. We cannot underestimate the influence of inspiration. It fuels a child's dream to be impactful and successful. That inspiration is often gained by connecting with people and experiences.

Some students struggle with the ability to envision, plan, and deliver a bright future due to lack of exposure. If students can't see themselves or know others attending college or ascending the career ladder, they may not be able to reach those goals. There are no prescribed assistance programs or formulas to instill inspiration. It can be hard to give kids hope.

Through Camino Forward, we've found that we can inspire students and give them hope through the power of storytelling. By bringing speakers and their powerful stories to the students, we've married what they learn in the class-room with exposure to people and experiences. For example, it's one thing to learn chemistry and biology; it's another to listen to a doctor tell you about their journey through college, medical school, and residency programs so you understand the sacrifices, hard work, and rewards associated with that career. The story becomes even more motivating when it's shared by a storyteller students can relate to.

The stories our speakers share with the students provide true perspective from their journeys—not just the triumphs and good times, but equally important, the tribulations and hard times as well. They come from sources with credibility, relatability, and passion. Essentially, these stories give students road maps for their paths. And not just paths for college and careers, but also for life.

The stories gave context to the 8 Themes that surfaced during Camino Forward. These are the themes that teachers, administrators, and principals pointed out they constantly hear about from students, and data highlights these as well.

I fully understand, appreciate, and value the need for academic curriculum and tests. But I think it would be hard to find one of our students who was more motivated and inspired by taking a college entrance exam than through a story of one of our speakers. Although both have been known to bring tears to students' eyes . . .

Speakers

When I conceived the idea of bringing speakers to students to share their stories, I made one bold assumption: that I would find inspiring business and community leaders willing to participate. Turns out, my assumption was a safe bet.

So much is written about the challenges that young Hispanics face—employment, health, and education, to name a few. We don't talk enough about those who beat the odds. We don't celebrate them as role models or consistently use them as examples. I thought we could do a better job of that in our community.

We aim to find speakers with different careers, backgrounds, stages in life, and stories. We want a variety of experiences to be shared with the students. The format is casual and organic. There are no set speeches, just conversation. We ask that the speakers be honest and transparent. They are challenged to not only share the wins in their lives. Students learn just as much, if not more, from the speakers' losses.

The speakers always rise to the occasion. They deliver insights the students crave. They tell of situations that students wouldn't believe if they didn't hear them from the source.

I had no doubt the students would be touched and impacted. What I didn't realize is how much the storytelling would affect the speakers. It's highly emotional for them at times as they recount some of their finest and toughest moments. Each speaker admittedly confesses that the level of discussion is equally powerful for them. It's hard for them to share inner feelings and a level of vulnerability that many have not tapped into for years. Some speakers even remark that it's the toughest public speaking they've ever done.

During one interview session with our speaker, Leticia, I asked if she would do anything differently in her life. She froze. She couldn't speak. I saw her eyes tear up. I quickly diverted and asked another question. After the session with the students, she told me that as she was thinking about her answer to my question, she went through a flurry of emotions. She couldn't get the words out. Leticia's path to college and a career in marketing and as a public relations executive has been successful but not easy. It's as if in that brief moment of questioning, a lifetime of sacrifices, hardships, and challenges came to her mind. She had no problem talking about her successes, but she had never really been asked to address her tribulations.

It made me appreciate that this was hard for our speakers, yet equally beneficial and rewarding as it was for the students. Our speakers need this time to reflect and share as much as the students. It helps remind them of where they've been, where they are, and where they're going . . . while helping others along the way.

I close each session by asking the students to give the speaker a round of applause. I urge them to understand that our speakers have had many accomplishments to be proud of, but that they also had tough times in their lives, and their perseverance and fortitude carried them through these. I tell the students to keep in mind that, just like the speakers, the toughest challenges they experience now will be the things they are most proud of in the future. I ask them to realize that not only do they have family and friends who want them to succeed in life, but they also have a community that wants them to do well . . . including our speakers.

While our speakers may be really busy all day, every day, they willingly meet with the students to share their life stories. They want to take time out of their schedule to speak to the students because they think it's important to do so. And like these speakers, our community is investing in and relying on the students to make a difference and do great things.

And without hesitation, the speakers are always quick to add that they should be the ones thanking the students for the opportunity to speak to them.

Students

It seems that Austin is on every top 10 list nowadays . . . best place to work, live, and, of course, barbecue. Our city has experienced tremendous growth over the last 10 years. It's an exciting time for our community. However, we still face challenges.

When I moved to Austin, it didn't take me long to realize that it was a tale of two cities divided by a major interstate, I-35. The west side of I-35 is considered the more affluent area, while east of I-35 has higher levels of economic disparity. Today, I live in West Austin. However, my life growing up was more like pockets of East Austin.

Children in these communities of East Austin live just miles away from one of our nation's top universities, the state capitol, and thriving businesses downtown. But they might as well be a universe away. Most of these kids cannot grasp the idea of a college education, voting in the legislature, or working in an office building. Many of them have never seen these landmarks firsthand or anyone who represents them. How can they dream, much less plan, to go to college, represent their community, or be a company executive if they don't know what that means or takes?

If we want students to pursue education and careers, we have to show them what that looks like. We have to expose them to places and people who portray these ideals. We have to let them walk on a college campus so they can feel the academic energy around them. They need to stroll the capitol hallways to understand public service. There has to be a conversation with an entrepreneur for them to appreciate the innovation behind starting a tech company. These are the experiences and conversations that will drive them to further their education and plan a career.

If these students don't have the opportunity or access to see these places or meet these people on their own, we have to bring these experiences to them. That's what we set out to do with Camino Forward. We want to expose the students to the individuals who can talk about the places and people who can shape their education and careers.

It was a concept that aligned well with the programming at some of our local schools as they initiated college and career-ready courses. In the classroom, they were instructing students on the process to go to college and build their resume. However, teachers and principals told me they fell short on giving students real-life examples of what it means to go to college and develop a career. That's where Camino Forward could help with speakers.

The majority of our students in East Austin are Hispanic. They're the ones I had in mind when I started the program and lined up speakers. The classrooms include a blend of White, Black, and Asian students. I wondered if the stories of Hispanic speakers would be well-received by such a diverse group. I soon learned that the students had mutual fears, concerns, and enthusiasm, regardless of their racial and ethnic profiles. They had similar challenges when it came to planning for their future. While they may not look or speak like the speaker in front of them, they could appreciate the lessons they shared. All the students need the additional support and guidance our speakers provide. This revelation prompted us to invite other diverse speakers to visit with the students as well, to expose the students to more insights and perspectives.

I've also thought a lot about the right age of students for this program. We want to have the ideal grade level in the classroom—not too young to understand the lessons or too old for them to lose interest. Turns out, there's no such thing on either side of the age spectrum. We've hosted classes with very engaged seventh and eighth graders. We've also had high school students through the twelfth grade. I think the program adds value to students well beyond high school as they go off to college and start their jobs. Since the stories of our speakers draw on experiences of a lifetime, there's something to be learned and applied at all ages.

The teachers, administrators, and principals I spoke with confirmed the need for Camino Forward. At times, I haven't felt that all of the students agreed. Some students are all in from the moment we introduce this concept and program. The minute the speaker walks up in front of the classroom, they're engaged, asking questions, and taking notes. Some students are quieter, never daring to raise their hand, but clearly absorbing every word the speakers and students share. Then, there's a portion of students who don't participate at all. It is almost as if they don't care or prefer not to be there. They're just going through the motions. They are a small percentage of the class, but it's the group that consumes me the most. While the students who are fully entrenched in the program inspire me, the students who are not connecting motivate me to constantly think of ways to evolve the program so all the students are engaged.

I always wonder if Camino Forward is helping the students. Is it being part of the solution? I need to know if it's positively impacting the kids. I thought I could see it by observing them in the classroom. But that's not enough. So I ask them.

At the end of the year, I ask the students for their feedback on the program. Some of the replies are compelling . . .[1]

"[It]made me not only reflect on my own story, but it made me realize that no matter where we come from or who we are, we are all willing to succeed, and these speakers are an example of that."

"[There's]nothing better than getting advice from people who already went through what we are now facing."

---

1   From letters to the author from students.

"[It introduced] me to speakers that were once in my shoes, showing me anything is possible."

"[I'm]learning of all the opportunities we have in life. That there's lots of people like us that thought they couldn't succeed in life or be someone important, and now they have become important in our society."

"[The] speakers came from rough backgrounds just like me."

"I want to change to become better."

The appreciation, recognition, and praise we receive from speakers, teachers, and school administrators is rewarding. But what really matters to me is the feedback from the students. I try to be realistic and understand that not every student we touch will be impacted by our message and program. Some may dismiss it or just not connect with our purpose. But I've seen and met enough students to know this is helpful for them and making a difference.

The students are why those who are part of this effort spend the time and energy to do it. So many of us feel there is a need for Camino Forward. The students have confirmed it. With a growing number of Hispanic students in our classrooms, in our communities, and across the country, the question I'm now asked the most is how to make the lessons from Camino Forward more accessible to more students.

At the end of each school year, I reflect on the program. I think about how we can improve and what the next steps are to grow Camino Forward. Students, speakers, teachers, and administrators have encouraged me to expand to other schools or other platforms to reach more students.

With just a few more sessions left to wrap up the most

recent year of the program, I was already excited to explore the next phase of Camino Forward. That enthusiasm abruptly ended. On March 13, 2020, our schools closed due to COVID-19. We had to cancel the program for the remainder of that school year.

That summer, I had so many questions. How do we proceed? Can we continue as schools evaluate plans to open schools? The school environment changed, and external guests were not allowed to enter in the fall. Virtual learning became the standard. We couldn't find a way to plug in the program remotely. The uncertainties around schools would continue throughout the next school year.

I was at a loss for what to do next. I was frustrated, sad, and stuck. I didn't want to lose the momentum or impact of Camino Forward. But we couldn't deliver Camino Forward in the classroom for the foreseeable future. I had to think of a different and new way to share the lessons and learnings. I had to do something.

Throughout the years, I've heard some creative ways to share Camino Forward on new platforms—podcasts, social media, websites, larger venues, and even writing a book. All of them were intriguing to me. But the least realistic in my mind was writing a book. Me . . . write a book? Really?!?! I was the kid who struggled to read and write.

Over the last few years, the pandemic has altered the way of life for so many—especially for our students in our school system. I figured that if they had to adapt to a new way of learning, I had no excuse for not pushing myself to deliver Camino Forward to students in a new way. So I started writing.

I wrote in the morning; I wrote at night and on the weekend. Before I knew it, I'd written a book on Camino Forward.

In this book, I attempt to capture the stories shared, lessons outlined, and experiences revealed that can serve as a road map for students in our community and others. Writing this book also forced me to connect my life experiences related to our themes as anecdotal examples in the *Mi Camino* sections.

This book highlights a wide spectrum of personal experiences. Not every speaker or student shares the same life story (me included), but I've discovered there are common experiences we can all learn from. You may be able to relate to some more than others. Some may uniquely touch you, while others may seem distant. You may agree with the narratives and context surrounding the themes, or you may feel they are too generalized or not fully representative. I do not intend for my words to represent an entire community. My goal is not to write or speak in terms of the absolute. Rather, my commentary is meant to provide a summarization of some common perspectives while understanding there may be alternative viewpoints. We all see, hear, read, and interpret things differently. If this book sparks others to share their caminos, then we all benefit. If only one of the stories resonates with you, it may make a difference.

While I always prefer to tell students the "why" behind Camino Forward in person, I hope this book serves as an acceptable alternative . . . at least until I can see them in person again.

CHAPTER 3

REMEMBER WHERE YOU COME FROM

t seems inevitable during each of our sessions that our speakers advise the students to "remember where you come from." To some students, it's counterintuitive. They ask, "Why think about the past if we're here to talk about our future?" The speakers' comeback is simple, but it's one the students hadn't considered: It's hard to know where you're going if you don't remember where you come from. Understanding and appreciating your past also helps you plan your future.

I like playing a specific video clip for the students that frames this theme. In it, Justice Sonia Maria Sotomayor, the only Hispanic to serve on the Supreme Court of the United

States, encourages an audience by telling them, "Don't lose an idea of where you came from and what it gave you . . ."[2]

Where you come from impacts who you become. Our speakers point out that the "where" does not just refer to the place. Even though the neighborhood you grow up in will have a lasting impression, it's also about the who, the why, and the when. For example, the people around you, the chain of events that brought you here, and the point in time it occurred. These "who, why, when" scenarios have lasting implications on our speakers.

Our students listen carefully as the speakers share experiences and stories that demonstrate how remembering where you came from **serves as inspiration** and **shapes who you are,** while motivating you to **help others in your situation**.

Serves as Inspiration

Above all, our speakers share that remembering their roots serves as inspiration to them. Their grandparents and parents overcame obstacles and made sacrifices throughout their lifetimes that were meant to benefit our speakers' well-being and position them for opportunities their relatives never had. Family members before them put their children and grandchildren's futures above their own immediate needs.

Perhaps more impressive than the mindset of this

---

2   Sotomayor interview with Oprah Winfrey, March 24, 2013, https://www. youtube.com/watch?app=desktop&v=jqEHV_ciVY4.

generation were the conditions and challenges they had to overcome. Many came from homes and communities full of poverty, limited education, and poor healthcare systems. Meals consisted of food they had to gather themselves or could barely afford to buy, while portions were rationed so everyone in the family could eat. School was not always an option since kids were expected to work at a young age to bring in money so families could pay for necessities. Doctor visits were reserved for only the most severe health issues.

Even with these conditions, they found hope. They harnessed talents, passion, and *ganas* to lift themselves up and out of despair. They made their way to a new country so they might have the chance for their American Dream. They knew their path to a new place, new language, new home, and new life would force them to leave family and loved ones behind. They knew they would miss out on birthdays, holidays, and traditions, fully realizing they might never return, never see those faces or hear those voices again. They would live the rest of their lives missing and remembering their homeland.

Despite it all, they made these choices in hopes of a better life. They didn't know where their immediate next step or day would lead them. They just had the audacity to dream and the faith to pray they were making the right decision for themselves and their families. They arrived to their new country only to realize that once they made it their new home, they would face a new set of obstacles. While it may pale in severity to the situation back home, they had to overcome these obstacles to keep their dream alive.

Our speakers use these stories of sacrifice to motivate the students. When facing their own challenges, our speakers thought of the challenges their grandparents and parents endured. Often, they realized that their situation was less daunting in comparison to the struggles of their family members before them. Who were they to complain compared to those who really faced tough times? Rather than complain about what was wrong, they wanted to demonstrate gratitude. They wanted to work hard to succeed, to show family that the outcomes of their decisions were worth the sacrifices.

Our speakers share that they do all they can to keep that inspiration in the forefront of their minds and hearts. They keep pictures or family albums close by so they can pull them out when they need a jolt of positivity. One speaker shared that he always carries with him a coin and pin that represents family mementos; these serve as something he can always reference for motivation.

Our speakers, like so many other immigrant families, take pride in their role of advancing the family name and status. In just one generation, they could impact the trajectory of their family. Speakers see this as a tremendous opportunity. Some see it as a responsibility, while many also recognize the stress and burden it carried. Some parents and grandparents had an expectation that the next generation would go further than them—live lives they could only dream about and build a path of financial prosperity over time, with each generation contributing after the next. Some called it *expectation*; others called it *hope*. When asked by students if it was a lot of pressure, one speaker said, "I think of it as *inspiration*."

One speaker captured this sentiment of inspiration perhaps more than any other. Geronimo is a first-generation American and the son of migrant farmers. The work took the family from South Texas to the Pacific Northwest following the crop season.

This travel limited Geronimo's time in school. As a teenager, he worked during the day with his parents and went to night school so he could pursue a high school education. It was that conviction that ultimately led his parents to make a tough decision and sacrifice. They would return to South Texas so Geronimo and his siblings could stay in one school for most of the school year and move once. With the new plan, his family instantly gave up a much-needed source of income; his parents would have to overcome this missing income so their children would have the opportunity to be the first in their family to receive an education.

Geronimo went on to graduate from high school, college, and law school. But he never forgot what his parents sacrificed or the life they lived to provide for their family. Geronimo's parents are still migrant workers. Now, every year, Geronimo trades in his dress shoes for boots when he visits them in Oregon to help harvest the potato crop.

Geronimo was one of the first speakers during Camino Forward. The first time he spoke to the students, it was a week after returning from Oregon to help his parents. He told the students his story. As he reflected, the emotion overwhelmed him. We had to pause as he and the students wiped tears from their eyes (yes, I did too). When asked why he still harvested potatoes now that he has an office job,

Geronimo explained that being in the crop field gave him an appreciation for his family, his opportunities, and the legacy he is leaving for his own son.

I left that session wondering who was inspired more by Geronimo's family—Geronimo, his parents, or the students listening to his story.

Guest speaker Geronimo.

Shapes Who You Are

Our speakers have made it a point to be loud and clear when they tell students they are who they are today because of where they came from. Your roots and upbringing shape what you think, speak, eat, feel, and believe. Sure, you can change and evolve with time. But we all have a starting point that begins our journey.

The speakers always refer to the values they learned in their homes and neighborhoods. The pillars of hard work, responsibility, and loyalty are at the top of each speaker's list. They confess that not every family member always abided by them, but these values were the cornerstone of family stories and anecdotes. Grandparents and parents strived to lead by example. Pride was a hallmark of their families. However, life's twists and turns may at times call for a more realistic and humbling perspective. The reality is that their families were just one generation away from poverty. It's a stark reminder that family mottos included "provide" as much as "pride."

Most speakers start their talks by reflecting on their upbringing with fondness, and then their inevitable struggles come up. Some speakers lead by telling the challenges and obstacles they faced, because it's what they remember most. Our students learn that remembering where you come from is not always a positive connotation. It can be painful. Remembering doesn't have to always have a nostalgic fondness associated with it. It could also serve as a driver of what you don't want to relive again. But whether positive or negative, remembering past experiences will shape your future.

The toughest part for our speakers seems to be the pressure and stress that come with generational change. For some, it's tough to hear your parents wanting you to have a better life and more opportunities than they had, especially when all you do is idolize them. There's a sense of guilt that comes with those best wishes. There's also a feeling of stress and anxiety when your parents and families put so much weight on your ability to be successful—not because they want you to provide for them, but because they want to take comfort that their sacrifices were justified. While they may have had jobs that exhausted them physically, they want the next generation to use their minds to make a difference.

That's what the students picked up on when Luis spoke to the class. His father opened an auto parts store in South Texas. By Luis's account, his father worked hard, took pride in his business, and enjoyed his job. However, it was not what he wanted for his children. He was adamant that someone in the family was going to college to have a chance for a brighter future and more opportunities.

Luis listened and went to college. A degree in corporate finance did not have the clout he expected, especially since he graduated during a banking crisis when no financial institutions were hiring, so he had to change his plans. At the random suggestion of a friend, he went to Washington, D.C., and applied for any job opening he could find. He returned to South Texas feeling exhausted and defeated. He thought he'd failed in his job search. But when he arrived home, there was a message waiting for him with a job offer. Luis moved to Washington, D.C., maximized his opportunity, and leveraged it into a career in politics and policy.

Luis has advised presidents, governors, senators, and congressmen. They all saw in him the same thing his first employer noticed when they offered him a job. Luis is personable, hardworking, respectful, and loyal—all traits he learned from his father working long hours at the shop. Luis's father may have wanted him to have a different career path. But it's what Luis learned by watching his father in his work that shaped him to actually make it happen.

Guest speaker Luis.

Our speakers take comfort in the notion that they are empowered to control their future. They can honor old traditions, adapt to new cultural norms, and create new ideas. That's the essence of remembering the past so it can shape who you become.

I always find myself paying close attention when speakers and students interact about how their surroundings have shaped them. Perhaps it's because my upbringing in the family restaurant business molded me in so many ways. My father, grandfather, and uncles all owned restaurants. So, at a young age, I started working at their restaurants.

My dad's restaurant is where I spent most of my time. I started in the kitchen with food prep, washing dishes, and trash duties. I graduated to bus boy and then waiter (lucky me, I kept my kitchen duties as well). Later roles included bar backing and valeting cars. And that was just on days we were open. On days the restaurant was closed, I swept the parking lot (I still have calluses from the wooden brooms), trimmed bushes, and pulled weeds.

Despite my family's constant reminder that "working" was good for me, I didn't believe them at first. Truthfully, it took time for me to appreciate the lessons I learned and the values instilled from working in the restaurant. I witnessed hard work, learned how to interact with people, and came to appreciate the value of a dollar.

In many ways, the dynamic of a busy night at the restaurant represented my life. In the kitchen, it was loud, yelling in Spanish, no diplomas, and financial struggles. In the dining room, it was quiet, conversations in English, college degrees, and wealth. Fortunately for me, I became comfortable in both settings. The restaurant prepared me for the surroundings I would experience throughout my life.

Working at the family restaurant with brother (left)
and father (middle).

Help Others in Your Situation

The challenges our speakers face are not unique to them. Generations of Hispanics and immigrants have lived these struggles. The United States has a long history of immigrants from around the world facing and overcoming obstacles to reach their dreams. But what is common among every generation of immigrants, regardless of their origin, is the inherent sense of obligation to honor the commitment of those who came before them.

It's clear that our speakers struggle with making good on that commitment. How do you repay those sacrifices made for you? It's not just about getting *your* education and landing a job that pays *you* well. What the speakers share is the desire to repay the sacrifices made for you by helping others in your situation. You should do your part to make sure others who identify with your struggles have the opportunity to overcome them as well. You must pay it forward.

For many, that means paving the way for your family. In our culture, family often has a long reach. We have more *tios*, *tias*, *primos*, and *primas* than we can count. So that gives us a great starting point. However, the helping hand must extend outside of our families as we assist our friends, neighborhoods, and communities. Many feel the more we help, the better.

This was a guiding principle our speaker Deanna lived by growing up in a small town where everyone knew one another. As a close-knit community, they considered everyone family. They celebrated one another, but more importantly they helped one another. While Deanna loved her hometown, she was also excited to leave for college and have new experiences.

But she kept her values and remembered what she learned at home. She never thought she was better than anyone. She treated everyone with respect and as an equal. She helped people up and pulled them in.

Her humanity and support for others were noticed by her peers and her employers. She rose through the ranks in the energy sector to become the President and CEO of a company. She may be sitting in the C-suite now, but she continues to treat everyone as if she was still back home in her small town.

While most of us would think the concept is simple, our speakers recount experiences to the contrary. In multiple cases, they talk about the unfortunate reality that what they often witnessed in their Hispanic communities was discouragement. The term *crabs in a bucket* was used to describe how some within the Hispanic community prevent one of their own from reaching the top to escape for a brighter future. They are often targets of jealousy, frustration, or anger unfairly directed at them.

Rather than pulling one another down, we need to help one another up. It's a belief that "all boats rise with the tide," as one speaker put it. The success of one family member or community member leads to the success of others.

So many of us draw strength from our families and communities. We must be sure that inspiration and help are there for those coming after us and that we pave the way for them. If one generation's burden is to start a path, the next must maintain it so those following can expand it.

I believe in this guiding principle. In fact, I've had to live it. It snuck up on me. My brother, Jose, and I are five years apart. Perhaps like most brothers, we fought . . . a lot. But we loved each other even more (not that we would tell each other that growing up). Our relationship became even more strained in the immediate years after my father passed away. Jose was in high school; I was in college. He was doing things I didn't approve of (although I did many of them as well). While he talked about college, I didn't really think he would go. Despite my nagging and repeated lecturing, I felt that he didn't take school seriously enough to get into college. When I felt I'd had enough of his antics, I told him and my mom that he was on his own. *Good luck getting to college*, I thought.

While my words didn't seem to bother him, I felt satisfied I had done my part to try to help him get past high school. I had moved on and needed to think about myself—to finish my degree and find a job.

Then my mom called. "Miguel . . . your brother needs your help." He wanted to go to college. Time and the opportunity to get there were running out. By then, I was feeling overwhelmed in my own life. I wanted to focus on my path. Besides, I had already tried to help him and felt more inclined to stay on the sidelines and watch him not get into college so I could say, "I told you so." That's right, I could be the crab that pulled him down. But while my mom said my brother needed help, what I really heard was *her* plea for help. And as the students know, when your *madre* asks for help . . . you help.

During my brother's last year of high school, we spent countless hours working on college applications and essays. We wrote personal letters to admission officers. Meanwhile,

I doubled down on my efforts at my school, Florida State University (FSU). I told any university representative who would listen that my brother should be admitted.

I remember the critical moment when we secured an in-person interview for my brother with an admissions officer at FSU. We went together. I'm not sure who was more nervous, my brother or me. The weeks we waited for notice were grueling. What would be his fate? Finally, the letter came . . . Jose was accepted to FSU. Through that experience I learned that wanting to help is not always easy. But when you help someone, it's not just rewarding for them. You get to enjoy their success as well.

Mi Camino

When I remember where I come from, I have mixed emotions. Today, I'm so proud of the "where, who, why, when" I experienced. But during my upbringing, it wasn't as clear. I struggled with my identity. Should I speak English or Spanish? Did I prefer arroz or hamburgers? Did I want to play soccer or football?

It took time for me to understand and appreciate the dichotomy a first-generation American lives is the richness of the opportunity. Like our speakers, I'm able to look back with fondness and recognize how my upbringing shaped me into who I am today. However, some of it brings back guilt, vulnerability, and shame. Primarily for me, it was the struggle over financial stability.

When my parents found their way to the U.S., they were high on hopes and dreams but low on cash reserves. They started a family and restaurant with savings my dad created by working in restaurants and hotels. My dad was not just a hopeful immigrant, but also an aspiring small business owner—an eager entrepreneur.

Throughout his decades in the restaurant business, there were some financial successes. The restaurant business provided some rewarding years for my dad and our family. I wore nice clothes and had the latest shoes. We ate at nice restaurants and traveled to Spain to see family. My parents not only provided for us, but they even spoiled us at times. My dad chose to spend his hard-earned money to enjoy life with vacations, food, and experiences.

But I also remember financial struggles, especially during my dad's later years. The spoils and luxuries came at the cost of other expenses. Perhaps they even masked a more humbling reality: My family didn't make saving or investing a priority. With time, as the restaurant business slowed down, we spent less on things and planned less for the future. I think we lived with an illusion that the business would turn the corner or that we could even sell the restaurant for a profit. Neither of those scenarios played out. Instead, my dad's passing left us few options and without financial security.

For many years, I didn't think much about our financial situation; nothing gave me reason to. Or maybe I was just too young to know. Yet, as I reached my teenage years, I became more aware of our socioeconomic status. I noticed how and when our family spent money. I listened to the late-night arguments between my parents about money. I saw the stress on my parents' faces when I asked for lunch money. As the years went on, our trips were limited.

My mom started cleaning houses for additional income. Our shopping was more prudent. (I can't tell you how many times I heard the Kmart loudspeaker announce a "blue light special"—and yes, I know some students may have to google "Kmart blue light special" to know what that means.) And when we achieved our family's dream of buying a house, it wasn't long after that I realized it was a purchase we really couldn't afford.

My parents made the investment in a house toward the end of my time in high school. Prior to that, we lived in apartments. About fifteen of those years were in an apartment complex called The Seasons. Let me tell you, nothing about this apartment complex development resembles the luxurious hotel chain that carries a similar name. What started as a charming community when my parents first moved there turned into a questionable neighborhood. Police car visits increased. The community pool attracted some shady characters. The laundry room required you to stay close by if you wanted to keep your stuff.

By my sophomore year in high school, guys who had just finished or dropped out of my high school were moving in. I remember when they held parties, I would sit in my room with the lights off and peek through the blinds to look across the parking lot at faces I recognized, including girls in my grade. I was scared to leave my apartment at the risk of being noticed. Whether it was the inconvenience of a long drive in the complex that led to my apartment or the hesitation of driving in the neighborhood, my friends and their parents would often skip pulling into The Seasons and drop me off behind the apartment complex. Then, I would walk through "the woods" to my place.

"The woods" was really just a thin barrier of trees around the apartment development. As a toddler, the woods provided a place to make forts and explore. By high school, it was a refuge for beer cans and some unruly late-night behavior. If my ride actually drove me to the bottom of our two-story apartment division, where we lived on the second floor, I found myself anxious to see what neighborhood spectacle we might witness that I would have to explain or laugh off to my friends or guests.

I discovered that using self-deprecating humor was sometimes the best method for explaining where we lived, if I couldn't avoid the subject altogether. The teasing and eyebrow raising that came with living in The Seasons became too much to defend or explain. Whenever I could, I elected to walk home. And when others found out, I would make a joke about it to deflect the embarrassment I associated with living there.

The place where I lived was not the only source of financial insecurity for me. Where I ate was as well. As our family finances diminished, we qualified for free school lunches. At that time, everyone knew who was receiving a free lunch because they were the only ones who didn't have to pay cash in the school cafeteria. I was mortified of being in the lunch line with friends and having to disclose that I received free lunches. For years at lunch period, I would make up excuses that would ensure I'd be the last one in the lunch line. That way, no one was around and could discover my meal was free on the perceived basis my parents couldn't afford it. It was a plan that didn't always work. Sometimes when I waited too long, the line was already closed, and I stayed hungry for the rest of the day. Other times I found myself with just minutes to eat before the lunch break ended. If I didn't make myself sick from eating so fast, I was late to my next class.

Thinking about some of my surroundings and circumstances, especially my family's financial situation, led to questions, anxiety, confusion, frustration, and embarrassment—the same emotions many teenagers face. I often blamed those feelings on being a first-generation American. I faulted my Hispanic roots for the tears of anger and sadness I would shed at night.

It took me time to realize that those feelings were not fair or just. What my family could or could not afford shouldn't solely define my life. It shouldn't outweigh the blessings and fortune we had or undermine the good. Rather, I could look at all my experiences growing up and allow them to shape my future and inform the path I take. I could re-create the positives and change the negatives; that ability was within my control.

Early on, it was easy to see what we had. As I got older, I started realizing what we didn't have more than focusing on what we needed. But through it all, I never felt my family was poor or that we went without. Rather, we were rich in many ways. The love and support my parents provided was the real treasure for our family. The morals, values, and examples they bestowed upon my brother and me is their legacy.

It wasn't about the money they made or spent; it was how hard they worked to earn their money. That's what I'm most grateful for. Our speakers would tell you the same.

When we create a path, we often think about starting that journey from our current position. In doing so, we fail to recognize the steps leading to it. We should think about our individual path as a continuation of our collective family path. If we do, we can learn from the past as we create our future, for ourselves and for our families.

Justice Sotomayor understood it. Her quote that I share with the students ends with, "But then go off on your rocket ship and explore the world and the universe."[3]

This "remember where you come from" mantra is the pillar of the lessons shared by our speakers and has become the theme that serves as the foundation for the following chapters.

---

3   Sotomayor interview with Oprah Winfrey, March 24, 2013, https://www. youtube.com/watch?app=desktop&v=jqEHV_ciVY4.

CHAPTER 4

FAMILY MATTERS

One of the most provoking questions the students ask our speakers is "Did your family support you?"

When it's asked, nearly the entire class sits forward, listening with attention. Clearly there is something to that question. As the speakers answer, it's obvious it's a heavy topic for discussion that weighs equally on the minds of speakers and students.

As might be expected, family is indeed a big part of each speaker's life. It's a focal point when they tell their stories. When we discuss family, the depth and passion with which speakers speak and students listen is captivating. It's simple and special in some ways, yet complex and messy in others. It warrants more attention.

The theme "Family Matters" was not part of the original program we shared with the students. But with each year, it's become more of a topic of interest. It sparks emotion and feelings—not all positive. So when I was writing this book, I knew I had to include it as its own chapter.

As the speakers remember where they came from, it's clear that their family is core to shaping and molding them. It's often what they talk about the most. They highlight their family **adapting to a new normal**, describe the **limitations** they experienced, the **generational change** they faced, and the **degrees of support** they received from their families.

Adapting to a New Normal

Our speakers tell stories of how one day their family was in one country, and the next day they were in the U.S. They would leave a pueblo, city, or country their families knew for decades, having been rooted in one place for generations. That's all they knew and perhaps all they wanted to know. Yet circumstances and dreams prompted them to leave it all for a new country. Some speakers moved after years of planning, while others talk of having to move suddenly, within minutes, due to necessity.

Once they stepped foot on new land, these immigrants had to learn a different culture and language, meet new friends, and find jobs and a place to live. Some had a contact in the U.S. to help them navigate their new home and give them a point of reference that helped them adapt. Others didn't know a soul. They had to figure things out on their own.

Some newcomers were eager to try new foods, learn

English, drive a car, and meet their neighbors. For others, it took time to build courage and become comfortable enough to explore their new world and surroundings. Many immediately embraced a new home, while some couldn't let go of their native homeland. While many sought a path of citizenship, others never stopped counting the days until they could go back to their homeland. Some excelled, while others struggled.

It was all so new and different for them; it's hard to imagine the excitement and fear they felt if you haven't felt it yourself. These experiences were surely overwhelming and stressful. And as our speakers tell their stories of struggle as their families assimilated to a new normal, the students nod in agreement as if the stories resemble the ones in their own families.

One such experience is that of our speaker Maricruz. Maricruz grew up in South Texas in an extremely modest setting. Her parents wanted to escape the conditions around them in Mexico. They left their homeland with little means, and their financial struggles continued when they moved to the U.S. There wasn't a dry eye in the classroom when Maricruz told the students that there was no guarantee of her next meal and described the way her family had to "search" for clothing.

Embedded in these newcomer stories are examples of families adjusting to change and underlying moments of inspiration that demonstrate connection to their new home. These moments include adapting to new traditions or perhaps new occupations during the early years of transition; these changes are now a hallmark of the family's identity. Starting businesses, taking trips, buying land, building houses, cooking meals, and designing clothes become some of the ways families adapt. In a sense, they are creating new memories and costumes for their next generations, ones that they couldn't make in their native countries.

In my family, one way we adapted was through sports. Football, not to be confused with fútbol (soccer in the U.S.), became our family's unexpected connection to our new country. My parents were not athletes or into sports. The only sport I saw my dad play with friends was racquetball. (I think he was into it more for the Mexican food and beers that followed than for the workout itself.) Soccer was my first sport, and I played it through high school. It was the sport my family in Spain and Canada passionately followed. However, American football became the common bond between our family stateside. At first, it was not the blocking and tackling that piqued our interest. It was tailgating!

On Sundays, my dad and his friends would drive an hour from Sarasota to Tampa Bay to watch the Buccaneers play in their home stadium. As my brother and I got older, we were invited to join them. My mom was invited, but she seldom came. (I think she viewed a Sunday without Poppy, Jose, or me as her own personal Super Bowl.) For us, the best part of the game was the pregame. We set up the best feast in the parking lot. No hot dogs for us—my dad brought *tortilla de papa* (a traditional Spanish omelet), smoked salmon, shrimp, and steak sandwiches. He and his friends would laugh and cook while the kiddos played football and innocently heckled the visiting team fans.

Inside the stadium, however, it was a different story. Our beloved Bucs team repeatedly had one of the worst records in the league. The only good thing for my dad is that he knew nothing about the game. Bad plays or penalties never bothered him because he didn't know what they meant. He just looked at the scoreboard at the end of the game for the final tally. The drive home consisted of me with stomach pain from the endless popcorn, pizza, and ice cream I'd eaten in the stadium. While my dad's friends complained about how poorly our team played, my dad just sat in silence with a grin on his face.

For him, it truly wasn't about the score or the team record. It was the experience. Here he was, in a new country, connecting with new friends, over a new sport, while creating a new experience for himself and his boys. Those experiences had a lasting impression on me. I continue to be a Tampa Bay Bucs fan.

Today, my son is an even a bigger fan, especially since Tom Brady, his favorite quarterback, joined the team. He watches the games with passion. He's in a great mood if they win and sad when they lose. As for me, I'm not nearly as invested in their wins and losses. I just watch with a grin on my face, thanking my dad for adapting and embracing.

I recently surprised my son with a trip to watch the Bucs play. We spent the day with my dad's friends. My son heard stories about my father, and we solidified a third-generation Bucs fan. The Bucs won the game in a thriller. I also felt like I won when, after the game as we left the stadium, my son said he would always remember the game. I replied, "You, me, and Abuelo Miguel!"

Attending Tampa Bay Buccaneers football games with my father.

Attending Tampa Bay Buccaneers football games with my son.

Limitations

While our parents and grandparents possessed the character-
istics they needed to overcome the hurdles they faced on their
way to a new land, they may have underestimated how much
they would utilize that same fortitude when they searched for
jobs, perseverance when they looked for a home, and patience
to learn a new language when they arrived.

Nothing could have prepared them for their new lives.
Neither the movies they watched, the books they read, nor the
songs they heard could adequately describe what it meant to
live in the U.S. as a Hispanic immigrant. There was little they

could do to prepare, considering that in most instances, they didn't know where they would settle. Regardless of the location, they quickly realized it was not what they expected—in both good and bad ways.

Think about it: Everything was new for them. They had to find a job, figure out where to send their children to school, and learn which doctors could take care of them. What about a home, utilities, transportation, and groceries? For us—the next generation that was born in the U.S.—these daily occurrences seem routine and take little thought. But for our family predecessors, they were points of frustration, fear, and helplessness.

The most difficult part for many was that they had to do everything in a *new language*. Their ability to express themselves and communicate with others changed drastically. They were limited in what they could say and to whom they could say it. Many adapted over time. They took English classes if schedules and money allowed. Others picked it up reading the newspapers, watching television, or communicating at work. While it wasn't perfect, their command of English helped them flourish in their new country.

Of course, many would never master their new language completely; their accents revealed their roots, and their writing was fraught with misspellings. Others in our families made even less progress. Whether because of mental roadblocks, lack of time, or native pride, they never learned enough English to fully assimilate to a new life. What our speakers share in those instances are their family members' wishes for their children and grandchildren to not experience the same disconnect they lived through for years.

When our speaker Rolando told his tale, this really hit home for the students. Rolando's parents were from Mexico. Like many immigrants, they arrived with aspirations of prosperity. They found an opportunity for work in farming. Rolando joined them in the cornfields. He would wake up at 5:30 a.m. six days a week (Sunday was his day off) to put on trash bags so he wouldn't get wet from the dew in the fields. The days were long. He especially remembered his mom looking tired and stressed. The family struggled to stay afloat while Rolando had problems fitting in at school.

Fortunately, before it was too late, Rolando realized that education was his way of not repeating his parents' struggles. He went on to graduate from college while serving in the U.S. Air Force, and he's currently worked for the City of Austin for over 10 years. Rolando has served his family, community, and country in ways that his family could only dream of. He wasn't going to fall victim to the same limitations that saddled his parents.

Rolando's story reminds me of what happened in my family. My grandmother, my mom's mom whom we all affectionally called Mama, was the matriarch of our family. When she and my grandfather, Pepe—he insisted everyone call him by his nickname, including the grandchildren—made the move from Spain to Canada, Mama had to adapt for herself and their five kids. My mom and her siblings picked up the English language with varying fluidity. Her youngest sister and brother assimilated the easiest since they were young enough to learn as children. Mama, on the other hand, never picked up English. In her 40 years in Toronto, she was not able to carry on a conversation in the language. When shopping or commuting, my grandmother just pointed and spoke slowly in Spanish. There are countless stories about Mama's miscommunication at stores, restaurants, buses, and trains. Some moments made us laugh, while others left us scared for her safety.

It's a family mystery why Mama never picked up the language. There are multiple theories: She didn't have the time. She was too proud (or too stubborn). It was too hard. She was scared to fail. She was embarrassed.

Regardless of why, the language barrier was a constant frustration for her. Despite our best efforts to speak Spanish when she was around, English would inevitably creep into a story or joke that we'd need to translate for her, after others had laughed at the punchline. She missed out on understanding school events, restaurant menus, movies, television shows, and public events.

I think this weighed on her over the years. Mama was vocal, with a standing presence in our family gatherings. Outside, she was quiet and reserved. As she grew older, she became more dependent on her children and grandchildren for translations. Her limited language skills prevented her true persona to show through. She often felt left out and isolated.

Mama passed away several years ago. I can't help but think that one of her regrets was not learning the English language. Observing Mama's struggles motivated my mother to further adapt and learn English once she settled in the U.S. She didn't want to be limited like her mother was.

Similar to my grandmother, my mom had few family resources to support her in her new environment. She had children to raise in a country where English was the dominant language. And she had her own anxieties and insecurities with her proficiency in English. But the way my mom sees it, she really didn't have a choice but to learn English. In Florida, she didn't have the luxury of private tutors or classes. She took some lessons at the local vocational school, but never consistently. Rather, she learned English with her children. She watched TV shows with us. She attended our sports events. She reviewed our schoolwork. I remember that one of my earliest homework assignments in elementary school was to provide definitions for a list of words. I assure you I was the only one looking them up in an English and Spanish dictionary so my mom could help me while she also learned at the same time.

Recently, my son brought home a reading and writing assignment and asked me for help. When I walked him through the answer, he said, "That's not how we do it at school." His comments reminded me that I, similar to my grandmother and mother, struggled with English. However, I realize I don't have to see it as a limitation. Rather, as I reflect on the sequence of adapting from my grandmother to my mom to me and now to my kids, I view it as an opportunity to learn and grow with each generation.

Generational Change

Students hear countless stories of parents and grandparents who migrated to the U.S. and experienced journeys loaded with struggles. But the struggles didn't discourage them to the point of giving up. What kept them fighting and persevering was not just the optimism of immediate positive changes; more important to them was the long-term generational impact they could have on their families for decades to come. They figured that if they could make it and survive, they were positioning their family for short-term stability and long-term success for the next generation. They understood how one generation could determine the trajectory of their family's future.

It was not just "hope" these families were chasing. They set expectations for each generation. Parents were candid with their children that they wanted them to have better lives. They wanted them to get an education and have careers in ways that parents could only dream of. They wanted more for them.

Their message was clear. By knowing family struggles, sacrifices, and expectations, how could their children not feel a sense of gratitude and obligation to their predecessors? But as well intended as these expectations were, they were met with some reservations by the next generation. Often, the hope and expectations set by the family came with the burden of pressure. Some families are betting on the next generation to financially take care of them; others want to take pride in knowing their sacrifices were justified. They may see it as the next generation's responsibility to ensure it was worth it and repay the family debt.

Two stories from our speakers really resonated with me and demonstrated the significance of generational change. Veronica grew up in El Paso, Texas. Her academic career led her to The University of Texas at Austin, then Yale Law

School. Just years after graduation, she worked at the White House as a policy advisor to the President of the United States. When speaking with the students, Veronica summarized the opportunity and trajectory of her family with a powerful comparison of generations. She pointed out that their path went from their grandmother cleaning houses to her granddaughter working at the White House.

Then, I think again of Maricruz. Her family's hardship weighed on Maricruz's mother to the point that she pleaded with her daughter to empower herself not to live the same life as she had. Maricruz was devastated by the reality that her mother's future was limited, while Maricruz had all the opportunity in the world. That plea was never lost on Maricruz. She delivered on the family expectation as she graduated from college and launched a career in international diplomacy and politics.

Veronica and Maricruz certainly changed their families' paths. Now one question remains: What will their children and grandchildren choose?

Degrees of Support

So many of the family stories we hear from our speakers are inspiring, positive, and courageous—but not all of them. We also listen to tales that dampened the spirits and tested the resolve of our speakers.

The degrees of support our speakers received from their families varied. Unfortunately, sometimes their home situations were tough—in some cases, downright disruptive and often painful. Your family may be the motivation and inspiration to move on to do great things, but it may also be the weight that prevents you from moving on. While we may want to relive some family memories, we might want to simply forget others.

Students hear plenty of uplifting family stories. But that's not necessarily what they want to or should always hear. More urgent to some of our students is not hearing how families lifted speakers up, but how they dealt with family and friends who tried to keep them down. What the students learn from our speakers is that sometimes family can hold you back by necessity, other times by personal feelings.

Speakers talk about how some families need all the help they can get. In most instances, the biggest need is money. It's simple: Without money, they can't afford the basics in life— food, shelter, electricity. They have to figure out how to provide for these basic necessities before they can plan for education, health insurance, and homeownership. To get there, everyone in the family is not only expected but also needed to earn money to cover family costs. In one household, grandparents, parents, and children might all work, regardless of age. These dire circumstances limit the growth and development of younger generations. How can they improve the family's long-term circumstances if they can't focus on the core skills they require to build a brighter future?

While this can be a devastating reality, we find that speakers in these circumstances are not necessarily resentful of their families. They know that their families were trying.

It isn't easy for parents to ask their children to make these sacrifices, consequently putting their future on hold. Parents, more than anyone, do not want the promises they make to their children of better lives to go unfulfilled. But it requires time to lay a foundation before they can build a family legacy. Patience is critical. Time is necessary before promises of a brighter future can be realized. When speakers were held back due to necessity, the experience left them valuing and appreciating opportunities when they finally unfolded. And when they did, they were even more determined not to miss their chance.

It's more frustrating, more difficult, and more complex to address family resistance when it's not planted in necessity, but rather through emotions and feelings. Our speakers at times felt that some family members were less supportive—discouraging them and negative about their plans and aspirations. In some extremes, they were threatening and abusive.

One of the most compelling examples shared came from our speaker Erica. She is a passionate, polished, educated Hispanic woman with a successful career that spans public service, higher education, and community organization positions. When she spoke, students listened. She engaged and connected with them as she shared her story as a girl in South Texas who'd been the victim of abusive conditions at home.

While Erica's family provided her basic needs of food and shelter, she did not feel cared for or supported. She questioned her value system and self-worth. Despite the disruptions she faced at home, she excelled academically. Her school support system provided the encouragement she needed to counterbalance the negativity in her house. When she graduated high school early, she picked up and left to remove herself from the unhealthy home environment in hopes of starting a new chapter far away.

Her teachers and counselors continued to stay by her side and pushed her to apply to college. They even got all the college application paperwork ready for her and walked her through the application process. They made it almost impossible for her not to complete and submit the application.

She was accepted and found herself having to make a decision. Should she continue her momentum of independence and find a job to start the career chapter of her life? Or should she pursue a path that she once wrote off—that of going to college and receiving a degree? Fortunately for her and others, she elected to go to college. Her career has skyrocketed, and the impact on others has amplified ever since.

Guest speaker Erica.

It's hard, perhaps unfair, to try to explain or understand family members' motives. We can only assume that the pressures and challenges they faced manifested in hurtful actions and words. Grandparents and parents may have had the best intentions to start new lives that would ultimately position their children for a brighter future. But when it was time for those dreams to become reality, they were met with hesitation, confusion, and doubt. It could have been sparked by fear, anxiety, or jealousy resulting from financial pitfalls, cultural norms, or family traditions.

The most frequent example shared by our speakers that demonstrates this experience is receiving an education, especially going to college. A common story goes something like this: Parents often spend years lecturing their kids about getting an education. They vigilantly monitored their classroom attendance, making sure they completed their homework and studied for tests. They asked to see their grades, dared them to dream about college, mandated that they at least apply. When they were accepted, however, everything changed. Optimism turned into doubt. Happiness changed to anxiety. Support was overrun by opposition. Once feeling they had an army of supporters, speakers found themselves on an island.

They were left to make the case to their loved ones that an education and college was not just their goal, but also a dream planted by their grandparents and parents. It wasn't just important to them, but critical for their family as well. It's not a "want," but rather a "need." In some instances, they were triumphant in making the case and renewing the support of their family. Unfortunately, in some cases, they're still trying to change the minds of loved ones.

Speakers share that maintaining the support of their family was not always easy. Not only did they have to convince themselves to take leaps of faith but they also had to persuade their family to join them. This was a challenging feat because their family did not fully grasp the opportunities presented. Parents knew they had reason to be proud of their first-generation kids; they often didn't understand exactly what they were proud of. For their children, succeeding was half the effort. Explaining it to their family was the other half. It could be exhausting and time consuming, but if done correctly, it presented a moment of pride to be understood, shared, and appreciated by the entire family.

For most of our speakers and students, the degrees of support were not always so extreme. Not every experience with their family was positive. Not every experience was negative. It seemed to vary day by day, week by week, or year by year. It depended on so many factors that surround their lives. That was my experience.

I struggled with the level of support from my family. Like our speakers and students, I knew there was underlying support for me. I never questioned their love or their motives, but at times I felt a disconnect between our perspectives. Perhaps the opinions that mattered most to me were those of the two men who meant the most to me: Pepe (my maternal grandfather) and Poppy (my father). They were the patriarchs who made the decisions to leave their home country for a new land of opportunity. They were the

most invested in ensuring my success and the two I wanted
to make most proud.

Each demonstrated their support differently. Pepe showed
his support with constant words of encouragement. He
wanted me to think bold and big for my future. He often said,
"Miguelito, tu vas hacer alguien en este mundo." ("Little Miguel,
you're going to be someone in this world.") Whether it was
good grades, scoring goals, or showing good manners, he was
the first one to smile, congratulate me, and encourage me to
keep up the great work. He may not have always understood
my success, but I knew I made him proud.

With Poppy, my father, it was more complicated. He not
only wanted me to have but also take advantage of every
opportunity he never had. His expectations were high. For
most of my life, I didn't know if I was meeting them. I didn't
always know how he felt. Because he was always at the restaurant, he never witnessed the school assemblies where I made
honor roll for my grades; he didn't attend many of my games
to see me score a goal, hit a home run, or make a tackle. He
had to experience it secondhand. I felt as if the notes from
teachers, newspaper clips, or reenactments from friends never
did the experience justice. My successes, motivated by him
in so many ways, felt as if they were falling short. He wasn't
able to see, and I wasn't able to explain their significance.
My frustration would build over time and eventually lead to
arguments—most of the time at Denny's.

That's right, the 24-hour breakfast restaurant. Denny's
was my dad's favorite place to eat after work. It was also one
of the only places you could eat that late. On Friday and

Saturday nights, when he would close the restaurant and bar, he would stop at Denny's on the way home, sometimes as late as 2:00 a.m. or 3:00 a.m. When I worked at the restaurant on the weekends, I would join him. The waitresses knew him by name and order (eggs over easy, crispy bacon, toast, and a glass of milk). I would order the Super Bird or Moons Over My Hammy. Our conversations always started with the night at the restaurant but then transition to heavy topics. We talked about my plans, my life, my future. He shared his life regrets and his expectations for me. They were some of the toughest conversations we had.

Often, they became heated. I felt my efforts were under-valued and unsupported. He surely felt underappreciated and misunderstood. Our raised voices and tears would draw attention (and that's saying something considering the cus-tomer base at Denny's at 2:00 a.m.).

When we got home, my mom would notice I was upset. (She always waited up for Poppy to come home from work.) She could tell the conversation weighed on me. She would say, "We only have one family. Your father means well and is proud of you." It was hard for me to believe that, coming from her. But I believed it when someone else told me.

One night, while I was working at the restaurant, a longtime patron told me how my father showed everyone in the restau-rant my "Player of the Week" photo in my high school football program. Apparently, he bragged about it to anyone who would listen. When I replied with skepticism, the same patron told me that Poppy was constantly showing everyone my report cards, awards, and pictures. It was clear to everyone who stepped foot in the restaurant how proud he was of me.

Yes, I wish Poppy could have told me directly. But he didn't or couldn't. But once I knew, it helped.

Justice Sotomayor has said that "it is hard to take your family on a new road you're traveling."[4] Just because it's hard, it doesn't mean it's not worth it. We may not always see or feel our family's support, but that doesn't mean they aren't proud.

Mi Camino

I think we realize how much family matters not when they're around but when they're not. I lost both Pepe and Poppy when I was young and had so much more to learn from them. They passed within just a couple of years of each other while I was in college. I lost two of my greatest inspirations. I was heartbroken, devastated, and demoralized.

They passed during some of my most formative and impressionable years. I felt they left when I needed them most. As if life wasn't tough enough when they were around, it became even harder with their passing, especially Poppy's. In short order, my personal goals were put on hold. No longer was graduating college and mapping out my career my priority. My attention now focused on my mother and brother. I had to take care of them.

---

4   Sotomayor interview with Eva Longoria, January 31, 2013, https://www.youtube.com/watch?app=desktop&v=B4PY9KV5DwA&spfreload=10.

The emotional, mental, and financial strains we faced were overwhelming and consuming. We had to learn how to live a new life together, a life without Poppy. How would we pay the bills? How would Madre find a job? Poppy managed all the family's finances. We had to start with understanding what we had and what we owed. We taught Madre how to pay bills and write checks. Much of this was new to me and foreign to my mom.

It was hard. There were days when emotions were hollow. Feelings were numb. Words were empty.

The hardest thing I ever had to do was give Poppy's eulogy. I don't know how the words came to mind to put on paper or much less how I found my voice that day at the church. As the priest acknowledged me, I walked up and took my place to give the eulogy. I looked up and realized the church was full of family, friends, and fans of Poppy. I gave my tribute. My eyes were dry. My voice did not crack. My knees did not buckle.

But the moment I left that church and sat in the car on the way to the cemetery, I cried. I mourned. I hurt. With those tears of sadness, some healing started. I not only thought about how much I missed him, but little by little, I also started remembering him—reliving fond memories, thinking of the lessons he and Pepe had taught me, remembering the advice they gave me.

If I was going to carry on with my life and help Madre and Jose, I had to remember Pepe and Poppy. Like them, I had to adapt to change. I had to continue my life without them by my side, but always in my mind and heart. What mattered most now was not questioning my relationships with them or their actions but cherishing the love and support they gave me.

When we think of our caminos, it's not just our path. Individually, we represent a small segment of a larger line—a family path that started before us and continues after us. What allows us to build a stronger and bolder individual path is our family. They accept risk and take on sacrifice so their children and grandchildren can have better lives than them. This act of humility and willingness to serve as a stepping-stone for others in your family and community is exactly the trait I want to take from my grandparents and parents and hope my kids will embrace.

And when they're ready, I look forward to taking my kids to Denny's to talk about my experiences, listen to their dreams, and prepare them for their future. Hopefully just over breakfast—hold the tears.

Because when my kids are asked, "Did your family support you?" I want their answer to be even better than mine.

CHAPTER 5

EMBRACE YOUR DIFFERENCES

During my first semester in college, I took a history class. Our big assignment was to write our own autobiography—a personal account of our life, with an imagined extension beyond our current age.

It was a tough assignment for me. At that time, I wasn't very comfortable talking about where I came from, and I had no clue where I was going (or wanted to go). I found myself revealing some personal accounts in my autobiography. I even had some fun with it and included a story about the infamous *cuchara de palo* in my home—that is, the wooden spoon that my mom would whip out so my brother and I would shape up.

I received an "A" on the paper. My professor even wrote a note that the cuchara de palo story made him laugh. When I showed my mom the paper, she had a much different reaction. She was mortified that I would share the cuchara de palo story. I guess she didn't see the humor as much as I did.

When we received our papers back from the professor, I read several of my classmates' autobiographies. I didn't see much overlap between my history and theirs. Definitely no mention of a cuchara de palo in their personal accounts! This wasn't the first time I realized how different I was from those around me. However, considering my professor's reaction to my story and my grade on the paper, it was one of the first times I thought my differences didn't hurt me. Instead, they might be recognized by others positively. It got me thinking that my differences were something I should acknowledge, be proud of, and share.

Madre cooking (minus the cuchara de palo).

Our speakers regularly highlight how they felt different throughout their lives. They share that their journeys were enriched when they stopped fighting or hiding their differences and, instead, embraced them. When our speakers encourage the students to embrace their differences, they express that being different is **hard but powerful**, is an **advantage, not a disadvantage**, to **share your story**, and to **connect with others with similar differences**.

Hard but Powerful

Students don't have to wait long to pick up on hints of how different speakers felt at times. The feeling of being out of place started when they were young, carried on through their years in school, and even continues today.

Speakers feel different because when comparing their circumstances to those around them, they realize that they speak differently, eat different foods, listen to different music, live in different homes, and look different. In some instances, they were bullied for these differences. Many were teased about their family income, their slow reading, the tortillas they ate at lunch, or the traditional clothes they wore. When describing their emotions related to these experiences, they use words like *insecure*, *ashamed*, *inadequate*, *embarrassed*, and *outcast*.

Despite the pain caused by the actions and words of others, our speakers didn't let those things define them. Rather, they speak of how they embrace these moments to motivate them. While they could clearly recognize the difference themselves, they still felt they could achieve what others had. The education, lifestyle, and luxuries . . . all were within their grasp. It may be harder or take longer for them to get there, but everything others had could be available to them.

It's hard to overcome the perceived inadequacies that come with being different, especially if others are piling on to what you already think. The resilience of our speakers gave them a new perspective. There was no reason to feel ashamed of their differences, but every reason to be proud of them. These differences are not what prevent your success; rather, they empower you to be successful.

An example we've shared with the students of how growing up differently can spark success is the story of George Lopez, the well-known comedian and actor. Lopez experienced a difficult upbringing. In his book, *Why You Crying? My Long, Hard Look at Life, Love, and Laughter*,[5] Lopez writes about his painful and harsh experiences and how he channeled them into comedy. He used humor to deal with his differences. It launched his career and demonstrated to other Hispanics that our uniqueness is an opportunity, not a burden.

It's powerful to see how our differences can make us feel vulnerable, then transform into a source of strength.

---

5   George Lopez, *Why You Crying? My Long, Hard Look at Life, Love, and Laughter* (New York: Touchstone, 2004).

An Advantage, Not a Disadvantage

Considering some of their experiences, our speakers used to think of their differences as disadvantages. They felt they were limited in growing or accomplishing because their differences were holding them back. What our speakers make very clear is that what they thought were disadvantages at the time ended up becoming advantages in the future.

Our differences are best thought of as our differentiators. Our personal history and experiences, and those of our family, set us apart. They allow us to see things through a distinct lens and give us a unique perspective. That ability to bring a new outlook is what others appreciate. It adds value because others don't see things the exact same way we do. Our differentiators are not only valued, but also sought after by others.

Those differences may seem even more noticeable at various stages in your life. Our speakers recalled feeling instant disconnect in a classroom, in sports, or when they started their first job. The most awkward experience for most was when they went to college. Many of them left smaller towns and communities to move to large campuses. Taking their first steps into their dorms and classrooms was daunting. They often didn't know or connect with anyone. Feeling out of place may not have been a new feeling, but this was on a bigger scale and on a new stage. Many coped by keeping their heads down and keeping to themselves to get through.

They learned they couldn't be silent or hide for long. Others approached them. Professors called on them in the classroom. Students asked them to join their study groups. Campus organizations recruited them. They were approached because others wanted a diverse set of opinions, experiences, and talents to be represented. Their differences were what got them invited to the table, not kicked out the door.

The differentiator with the most complexity for our speakers was language skills—specifically communicating in Spanish. Some speakers could speak Spanish; some could not. But all of them recognized the ability to do so as a huge advantage. Unfortunately, some were never taught, which is a consequence of how the language was viewed by others. Their families purposefully avoided Spanish to avert the stereotypes and negative connotation that came with it. Rather than continuing to speak Spanish in their home, some grandparents and parents instituted an "English only" policy so their families could better assimilate into their new country—so they would fit in and not be viewed as different. But many families now regret that decision.

Today, in a global society, knowing multiple languages is an advantage. Employers recruit and compensate individuals with extensive Spanish skills. Music, television, radio, digital media, and food industries are catering to audiences in Spanish. Families of Hispanic descent are well-positioned to teach Spanish in their homes and be beneficiaries of the advancement of the language's future popularity in their new land. Unfortunately, many elected to leave their native language behind because they feared the repercussions. They bypassed the advantage it could ultimately provide their families.

My family had the same decision to make. We spoke Spanish at home. I only began to learn English as I watched television and played outside with friends. When I started school, I was clearly behind other students in language skills. My speaking, writing, and reading skills lagged behind my native English-speaking peers. In first grade, my teachers suggested to my parents that we only speak English at home so I could better assimilate to school. Poppy said, "No way!" I'm not sure if it was his pride, stubbornness, or desire to have a bilingual family, but he told my teachers we would speak Spanish at home. He and my mom would work harder to improve my English skills, but dropping Spanish was not an option. It made school hard for the following years—for me and for my parents. Early on, I wished my teachers had won over my dad with their suggestion. But with time, I realized the advantages of being bilingual.

Today, it's a priority for me to have my kids speak Spanish. Circumstances have flipped and now English is the dominant language in our home, so we work at learning Spanish. In fact, my kids use the same dictionaries my father used to learn English, but now to learn Spanish.

Family dictionaries.

Almost every night, we read in both English and Spanish. We count in both languages. The first words my kids hear from me in the morning are "*Buenos días. ¿Cómo dormiste?*" ("Good morning. How did you sleep?") The last words of the night are "*Buenas noches. Te quiero.*" ("Good night. I love you.")

It's amazing to think how one generation felt they were punished for speaking Spanish and the next feels they will be rewarded.

Share Your Story

Our speakers were best positioned to leverage their differences for positive gains when they understood them, embraced them, and knew how to explain them. Some of them learned the hard way that they should be able to talk about their differences. They faced uninformed, uneducated, and false assumptions held by others. People thought they knew everything about them without ever talking to them. They were stereotyped by neighbors, classmates, teachers, and coaches. They had to push back and correct these misrepresentations. They had to let others know the truth and understand the realities. They had to personalize their experience. They had to share their story.

Before you can share your story, you must know and appreciate it. You must understand who you are and where you come from. Speakers recall listening to their grandparents and parents tell stories about their roots, homeland, and new home. They held tight to memories of what they saw, heard, and smelled growing up, like waking up to the smell of Abuela's cooking, dancing the night away at a family wedding, or singing *feliz cumpleaños* at birthdays.

Once you grasp the uniqueness and richness of your story, you're equipped to tell it. But that's easier said than done for most of us. It takes nerve to share parts of who you are, especially if you've been embarrassed about it in the past. Many find that it's easier to start by sharing with one person at a time. As your confidence increases, you feel emboldened to tell others. Then you find yourself telling whole groups. Every occasion enlightens others who previously had no idea what it meant to be in your shoes, or in the shoes of others like you.

The actress America Ferrera, whose parents are from Honduras and immigrated to the U.S., captures the essence of sharing one's story in a way that resonated with the students when we shared her quote, "I feel like my convictions and my passions come from my very personal experience and the life that I've led. I feel the very natural tendency to stand up for and use my voice for the things that I know about and the things that I feel passionate about."[6] She has successfully done what our speakers preach to our students—that when you know your story, you can share it to educate, advocate, and drive change for yourself and others.

As we travel on our life paths, we may find ourselves to be the only Hispanic on the stage or field or in the classroom

6   Drawn from a CNN interview with the actress: https://www.cnn.com/2012/08/23/showbiz/celebrity-news-gossip/america-ferrera-web-series/index.html.

or boardroom. Your story will be different from others. Be prepared to tell it. If done well, you likely won't find yourself alone for long.

Connect with Others with Similar Differences

There were certainly times in our speakers' lives when they felt they were on their own. They were lonely, scared, and sad without someone around them they could talk to, someone they could relate to. Someone who had similar triumphs and challenges. Someone who could laugh or cry with them depending on the circumstances of the day. Someone who shared their differences.

The obvious remedy for this sense of detachment was to find others they could connect with—clearly easier said than done. Speakers constantly talk about how different they were from others around them. How no one around them shared their experiences or background. This contradiction leads the students to ask, "How do you connect with someone like you if you're the only one that's different?"

The irony is not lost on our speakers, especially Yvette. Born in the Rio Grande Valley, not only was she one of the first in her family to go to college, but she was also one of the few in her high school class to go to college. She wasn't inspired by what she wanted her career to be; rather, she was motivated to leave the comforts of a small hometown to see new things and meet new people.

While she was eager to meet *new* faces, she didn't

realize how *different* those faces would be. She came from a hometown where she looked and spoke like her friends and neighbors. She was now on a university campus where she was the one who didn't fit in. She decided to change it. She found herself making her environment one that she and others like her could fit into and thrive. It's a passion she's developed into a career.

Other speakers acknowledge that during their journeys, they were often the anomaly in their settings. They were different from those on their sports team, in their classroom, or at their job. But that didn't mean there weren't others close by going through similar experiences and feelings. There may not be many like you, but when there are, you'll take notice. Keep your head up and you'll spot them.

Our common differences attract us to others. When you're in an unfamiliar setting and you hear a name that reminds you of a relative, you feel an instant linkage. When you're in the room and someone speaks Spanish, they pique your interest. At a restaurant, if someone orders a meal that reminds you of your family, you turn to smell the dish. Whether it sparks an awareness, a conversation, or a friendship, we take comfort in coming across someone we relate to in one way or another. With time, we may be pleasantly surprised by how many others we come across who share similar points of history, culture, or sacrifices. Understanding how your differences connect you with others may inspire you and lead to your success.

That was the case for one of our speakers, Miguel (I refer to him as "the other Miguel" to the students). Miguel was raised in Laredo, Texas. His parents raised him and his four siblings with an emphasis on education that led Miguel to graduate from The University of Texas at Austin, where he received his degree and went on to attend law school. His education gave him a solid foundation to explore various career opportunities. But his plans took an unexpected turn when his family set out to solve his sister's dietary restrictions.

Growing up, their family enjoyed traditional Mexican foods. His sister developed some health challenges that prevented her from enjoying her favorite meals. As a gesture of support, the entire family also changed their diet. But for them, tacos and fajitas weren't nearly as good on a lettuce leaf than on flour and corn tortillas. So Miguel's sister, Veronica, started making almond flour tortillas, even receiving their *abuela's* stamp of approval on the taste. Their heritage-inspired experience started a family business venture. Today, Siete Family Foods (*siete* for their seven family members) has grown into a multimillion-dollar food company.

When speaking with the students, Miguel uses his family's story and business as an example of how a family experience can connect you to others. The family thought their circumstances were different and unique to them. They had no idea how many others could relate to it. As it turns out, many share their need and passion for healthy and authentic Hispanic food. Starting a business has given them a platform to not only connect with, but also to help others.

Guest speaker Miguel.

Mi Camino

I am proud of my family history. I understand that the struggles and challenges we have faced may positively shape our future. I recognize that the traits we perceived as weaknesses become our strengths. I realize that we have a responsibility to share our story with those who benefit from hearing it. I believe connection with others provides comfort and confidence through numbers.

I say this now. But I haven't always practiced and believed what I preach today. I used to hide my family story. Maybe not the headline of coming from immigrant parents, but the stuff beneath the surface. The tough times. The financial strains. I was embarrassed to share those realities. They made me feel too different from those around me.

One difference that I really got hung up on was where I lived. For most of my life growing up, we lived in an apartment. I really wanted to live in a house. Not just because all my friends did, although being the only one who lived in an apartment—especially the apartment complex we lived in—opened me up to jokes and ridicule. I wanted a house where I could feel stable and secure.

I can't say I felt safe every night when I went to bed. I asked, bargained, and pleaded with Poppy to purchase a house. Once he was old enough to start feeling the same way, my brother, Jose, joined me in the campaign to purchase a house. With time, my mom conceded and joined us. Finally, Poppy had no choice. He purchased a house.

It was better than I could have ever dreamed. Not only did we each have a room, but we had a guest room as well. We went from all sharing one bathroom to having three. The best part, we had a pool! I loved that house. It was warm, spacious, and comfortable. And it was ours.

The enjoyment of the house was relatively short-lived. Two years after purchasing the house, I went off to college. Three years later, Poppy passed. We sold the house two years later.

When Poppy passed, I had to take over the family finances. That's when I understood why it took us so long to purchase a house and why Poppy was so resistant. It's expensive! Most people require borrowing money to buy a home. For us, it was a lot of money. Without any steady income once Poppy passed, the financial burden was too much to maintain. We had to sell. And once again, I found myself living through something no one else I knew had experienced.

Years later, while living in Washington, D.C., and working in the U.S. Capitol, that experience drove me to make a change for others in that same situation. As a young congressional staffer, I worked on the legislation called the American Dream Down Payment Act. This legislation assisted first-time, low-income homebuyers on the path to homeownership by helping with down payments and closing costs so they could afford to purchase their own home. It was thrilling to be at the center of legislation that was signed by the President of the United States. However, it was more rewarding to be part of an idea to help others I could relate to—people who shared in our family's dream to buy a house yet faced the same financial constraints.

I could have easily shied away or hidden from that experience for the rest of my life. Instead, I embraced it. I allowed it to serve as a guiding pillar when given the chance to do something about it. My own experience empowered me to speak with authenticity. Others thought I was genuine in my motives because I'd lived the struggle and empathized with those who required this support and assistance. Because I embraced my differences, I was able to make a difference.

I remember toasting Poppy the night the bill was voted on. I think he toasted me from above when I purchased my first house. I think we toasted each other when I helped Mom pay off her new home and completed his path to homeownership.

Writing my autobiography in college was just the beginning of me writing about my differences. Today, I can fill more chapters.

CHAPTER 6

EACH PATH IS UNIQUE

As students embark on their journey through school and plan a career, it's common to have the impression it will be a straight-line trajectory. Kind of like this:

I know this, because I thought the same: Do well in school, get a job, and watch your life skyrocket. But our speakers point out to the students that for most of us, that's usually not how it works. Instead, their paths were more of a maze:

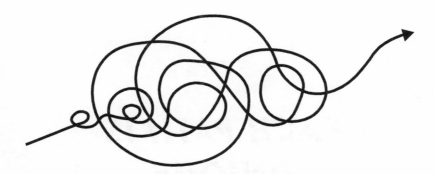

None of our speakers have lived a path that was a straight line. Rather, their paths included ups and downs and even circles. And no two paths have been the same. Each speaker's path was unique to them, full of distinct moments, decisions, and people that impacted their lives.

While their paths are unique, there were four common lessons they emphasized with the students based on their caminos: **know your "why," learn from others, adapt and overcome challenges**, and be ready for the **"fork in the road" moments**.

Know Your "Why"

Some speakers grew up being asked by their families and friends what they wanted to be when they grew up. Did they want to be a lawyer, doctor, or engineer? Some even came from families that expected them to take on a certain profession. But our speakers implore the students to challenge that conventional thinking. They want the students to ask not *what* they want to be but to discover *why* they want to be. Their view is that your "why" is your purpose and passion. Your "what" is the way you deliver and execute on your "why." There can be several jobs or careers that position you to fulfill your "why."

One example was a student who wanted to help people with their immigration status. The "traditional" view might suggest the career best suited to meet this goal would be a lawyer. However, a quick brainstorm indicated that a student with a "why" to help others with their immigration status could not only pursue a career in law, but also be a social worker, nonprofit leader, customs agent, diplomat, or elected official. The students grasped that identifying your "why" can lead to endless options for your "what."

The challenge that many of our speakers face was pinpointing their "why." Finding a passion to inspire a lifetime journey can be daunting and overwhelming. Our speakers' personal experiences often fueled their interests and career goals. Cultural foods can inspire us to be chefs, music from homelands creates musicians, taking care of grandparents prompts nurses and doctors, and solving family challenges sparks entrepreneurs.

Knowing your "why" not only drives you toward your path but also keeps you there. Students often ask speakers if they ever wanted to quit along the way. Speakers always say yes, absolutely . . . because it's hard. When students follow up and ask why they didn't quit, our speakers revert back to their passion, such as their desire to help others who are like them or remind them of their family.

Some speakers know their "why" early on. For others (including me), it takes longer. It's a matter of having experiences. Sometimes we find a career path by process of elimination—that is, discovering what we *don't* want to do. There's no penalty for finding your true passion after you've explored a few interests. In many ways, those trials secure a stronger connection to your "why" once you find it.

The path of Sandra Cisneros serves as an example that resonated with the students. The award-winning author publicly shared that she found her future because she "knew what I didn't want to do."[7] Ultimately, she found her passion in writing and telling stories. There weren't many Hispanic female authors who trailblazed the industry and served as role models for her. However, her success surely helped others find their "why" at many stages in their lives and careers. And while she may not have known how to become an author, her path serves as a fine road map for other aspiring writers.

By knowing our "why," it becomes easier to overcome the roadblocks of *how* to get there.

---

7   "Sandra Cisneros Looks Back as a Writer in Search of Home," PBS, October 29, 2015, https://www.pbs.org/newshour/show/bookshelf-2.

Learn from Others

As if it isn't tough enough to figure out your "why" and "what," you also have to figure out the "how." How do you pursue a career? A road map to a job from someone who's been there is a great starting point. If someone has achieved a career or job you want, you can learn from them. Study how they got to where they are. By understanding someone else's path, you can create your own. You can find out the education they received, the schools they attended, and the degrees they earned. You may discover where they worked, how long they worked there, and how many different jobs they've had. Pulling this information together about various individuals who have reached your goals will create an educational and career blueprint.

If you personally know someone who can share the way they achieved a career you are passionate about, you're fortunate. Take advantage of it and learn all you can from them. Be a sponge and soak in all you can. But for most of our students, the challenge is finding and learning directly from the individuals who own the road map.

You may be more comfortable looking for some guidance from those closest to you—your family members and friends. But in most instances, they won't know the way. Your limited reach, connections, and network mean that you may not know anyone who's done it before. The jobs you often desire seem unattainable because you don't know how to find the paths leading to them.

According to our speakers, that shouldn't stop you. The solution: Look outside your circle. It doesn't matter if you personally know someone or not; you can research their educational and career path. You might think it's hard to find this kind of information. While that may have been true in the past, nowadays it's readily available. Most professionals freely share their bios and resumes. They have personal and professional websites and profiles on platforms like LinkedIn; they write blogs or host podcasts. Some of them even provide contact information, welcoming questions, interactions, and the opportunity to share career advice.

The public domain serves as a valuable resource where you can learn from others. I personally know because I leaned on it heavily myself. If I wanted to be a restaurant owner, I could ask my dad, mom, grandfather, uncles, aunt, and a host of other family members how to start and manage a restaurant. It was our family's business for generations. But I didn't want to be in that business (or more accurately, everyone in my family knew how hard it was and urged me to pursue other careers). So I tried to find out more about other jobs—like being a lawyer, doctor, or accountant. My challenge was that no one in my family held those positions. I couldn't go to a loved one to learn about those jobs, much less ask for guidance on the career path to achieve them.

Like our speakers, I had to resort to some creative investigating to learn about various professions and what it took to achieve a career. I spent a lot of time studying how people in certain jobs got there. I tracked where they were born, their family history, where they studied, what they studied, and how they pivoted throughout their careers. I studied bios, listened to their interviews, read books, and tuned in to podcasts.

I could learn so much from these people by just observing their experiences and stories. I would start researching one biography in one industry, then end up 10 individuals later in a completely different role. I was discovering degrees, companies, and jobs I didn't even know existed. Not only was I learning from these individuals, but I was being inspired by them as well. The opportunities seemed endless, but more importantly, the paths to get there became clearer.

I still do this today. Anytime I find myself asking how to get to that career or job, I open up my LinkedIn account and start searching. Sometimes, hours later, after dozens of searches, I see the educational and professional road map. By learning from others, including those we don't even know, the possibilities for our own path becomes easier to see.

Adapt and Overcome Challenges

Our students hear plenty of success stories from our speakers. It's uplifting for them to witness these testimonies. I can see the transformation in their eyes as they become open to promise, potential, and vision. But equally important is recognizing the obstacles the speakers faced during their paths. Our speakers had their fair share of wins in their lives, but they also had plenty of losses. But it's their ability to adapt and overcome challenges that really molded their trajectory, more so than the accomplishments.

I can tell that some of our speakers are sensitive to sharing their failures. They don't want to overwhelm or scare the students with the imperfect parts of their lives. But their willingness to be vulnerable and share their challenges leads to some of the most meaningful and transparent lessons learned by students. It's the stuff that students may not want to hear but should hear. It's the examples of failing a class, almost dropping out of school, near bouts with police, clashes with parents, losing jobs, and denied applications that spark the most memorable exchanges.

No path is perfect. You'll undoubtedly experience mistakes, failures, and rejections. Each comes with varying degrees of impact, repercussions, and responsibility. Your ability to understand the circumstances, hold yourself accountable for your actions, and course correct not only remedy the current situation, but also provide guardrails for the future.

The critical points along your path correspond to the decisions you make. Poor decisions, or inaction, may lead to mistakes. Mistakes can get you off the right path. You can correct the path, but it may be hard and require more focus and commitment. Poor decisions can be made at any point in your life. You can also make up for them at any age. At least when you make a mistake, you can do something to correct it.

Experiencing failures and rejections can be harder. They are somewhat out of your control. They can be demoralizing because they make you feel that you aren't good enough. But once you get through the pain, you can grow from them, just as you can when you make a mistake. Sometimes, without realizing it at the time, you're better off long term when things don't go your way. Today's disappointment leads to tomorrow's joy.

Students heard how one speaker experienced multiple challenges in school and his career that required him to adapt and overcome to be successful. Carlos grew up in South Texas. He was a model student for years until he "got into a little trouble" at school. He playfully refers to the situation now, but at the time, it almost significantly altered his future plans. The incident dropped him out of the top 10 percent in his high school class—a distinguishing recognition that ensured his admission and funding to one of the state's top universities. Rather than panic and quit his plans for college due to the setback, he doubled down and was not only accepted into and graduated from college, but also rolled straight into law school.

After law school, he encountered another altering experience. Without a clear direction on what he wanted to do and scrambling for ideas for a job, he decided to take an idea from a "B-" paper he wrote in law school and turn it into a business plan. With little support and money, he formed a company. He ran up credit card debt to keep the business going.

Finally, things turned a corner. His naysayers became his clients, and the company made a profit. For 15 years, his company has grown, he's hired additional staff, and he's donated to dozens of causes in the community. All because he didn't balk when challenges presented themselves. Instead he let them fuel his perseverance and drive. In Carlos's mind, it's made him stronger.

Our speakers share varying examples of mistakes, failures, and rejections at different points in their lives. Some made the poor decisions of hanging out with the "wrong" crowd as teenagers, but then surrounded themselves with more positive influences before it was too late. Many were denied their top college choice but went on to receive scholarships and accolades from other universities. Several speakers got fired from one company, only to be hired by another for their dream job.

One recurring piece of advice speakers share is to not be afraid to make mistakes, fail, or be rejected. Instead of letting it get them down or push them away, they position these instances of adversity as learning moments and a stronger force of motivation.

As a University of Texas student, our speaker Lem finally made the basketball team after three years of trying out. When he made the team, his grades suffered and he was having a hard time balancing being a student athlete. Lem focused on his education and improved his grades. As he later started his professional career, Lem struggled for several years to adapt to new business cultures. Lem adapted by surrounding himself with individuals he could relate to and struggled just like him. With renewed support and perspective, Lem began to find success in the corporate world. That was when Lem landed a position as an executive for a cybersecurity company. He attributes his ability to overcome these challenges to not being afraid to fail. And when he did, he worked harder, kept his focus, and stayed determined to overcome the setbacks.

Guest speaker Lem.

As I listened to Carlos, Lem, and other speakers, I could totally relate. In my own life, rejection seemed to be a constant. One of the most painful came right when I was full of hope and optimism.

During my last semester of college, I sent out nearly 100 letters to companies expressing my interest in employment. I spent countless hours preparing my resume, typing up letters, and hand-stuffing envelopes. The result: zero job offers. Ouch! It was a gut punch and demoralizing at the time. But it forced me to rethink my plans and passions. Several months later, I applied to two graduate school programs. I was accepted by both. As it turned out, my career has been better off in the long run for it. Perhaps more importantly, it was good for me to experience the agony and heartbreak that came along with those 100 rejections.

Considering that our speakers (and I) have lived to tell our stories is proof that one can adapt and overcome challenges. The resilience, character, and focus that comes from this shows that we can actually win in the end even when we think we're losing along the way.

"Fork in the Road" Moments

One of my favorite interactions with our speakers is when we ask them to describe their "fork in the road" moment. That is, a time in their life when they found themselves at a critical juncture when making a key decision would send them down one of two very different paths.

While all paths are unique, we find that all our speakers experience these turning points. They occur at different times in their lives and under varied circumstances. For some, they had to make a decision between friends or future. Others had to choose between staying home or going to college. As our speakers look back at these fork-in-the-road moments, it seems to be an easier call with hindsight, as if the right decision was so obvious. But they are still the same fork-in-the-road moments the students face today.

What is most insightful is not that they had to make a decision, but how they made it. Sometimes they were forced to make decisions in minutes, with life-or-death implications. Other instances required a lot of time to discern and balance the feelings of loved ones. Regardless of the conditions or timelines, it's obvious that these fork-in-the-road moments are still fresh in their minds and carry high emotion.

The amazing thing is that in all the accounts shared, our speakers' lives improved with the decisions they made. That's not by coincidence. It's because they recognized the situation and the dire implications that came with their decision.

The decisions they made were often hard and humbling. Such was the case for Leticia (a different Leticia from the one mentioned earlier in the book). Leticia grew up in a community without a lot of Hispanic representation. She was the only Hispanic in her high school's honor classes. Despite her unique setting and some teasing from a pestering classmate who called her a coconut (brown on the outside, white on the inside), Leticia excelled. She was a leader in various school organizations, including head cheerleader and President of Girls' Interact, while also graduating as one of the top 20 students in her class. She was accepted to a leading university, and what made it even better, she received a scholarship. She did all the right things in high school. Leticia's fork-in-the-road moment came when she started college.

Like with many of our speakers, Leticia's arrival on her college campus was overwhelming. She struggled, lost focus, and confused her purpose. Consequently, her grades dropped, and she lost her scholarship. That's when she found her life at a crossroads. Rather than drop out of college and cave into shame and defeat, she chose a path that allowed her to reset and restart. She told her family about the situation. She asked for help and money to pay for college. She realized the gravity of her appeal, knowing how proud they were of her and their limited financial circumstances.

Nonetheless, they pulled together the dollars to get her what she needed to stay in college. A renewed and reenergized Leticia changed her priorities and interests. She graduated and went on to a career in legislative and academic affairs. Today, she helps students like her not only get to college but also stay in college and plan for a career. In Leticia's case, not only did her fork-in-the-road moment change her; it also has impacted hundreds of students.

Hearing from our speakers gives the students perspective into *when* they may face their own fork-in-the-road moments. But the bigger takeaway is *how* they should tackle and think about decisions that will impact their life—and the lives of others.

Mi Camino

As I listen to speakers recount their unique paths, especially their most fragile experiences, I can't help but relive mine. To this day, I often think about how and where I found myself going to college. It was a period of time when I lived a roller coaster of emotions and experiences. It started with potential, endured heartbreak, overcame fear, and landed on promise.

The journey began with American football. I was a fan as a youngster. I played football on the playground with the neighbors. I broke my arm during the neighborhood Super Bowl. My parents didn't let me play organized football until I was in the eighth grade. My nagging must have finally weighed on them, and they allowed me to play high school football as well.

Despite being a starter on defense and being moved up to the varsity team after my sophomore year, I questioned my skills. I was not the biggest or fastest guy on the team. Just before my junior year, I almost quit the football program. I doubted myself and second-guessed my commitment to play. Fortunately, friends, players, and coaches cared too much to let me abandon a sport for which I had potential. I focused on my strengths—preparation, hard work, and playing smart. I doubled down on my game, and it started to pay off in ways

I never imagined. By the end of my junior year, I received college recruitment letters. My confidence grew.

Football also created a stronger bond with my family. During my senior year, our local newspaper ran a feature article on me entitled, "Romano Embodies Riverview Tradition." The story not only featured my commitment to football, but more importantly to me, it also highlighted my family's journey and my appreciation for my parents. In the article, I'm quoted as saying, "Through [my dad], I can see how hard it is to be successful." Poppy said of me in the article, "He's a leader. I had to be a leader. I had to control my own destiny."[8] Considering that Poppy and I struggled to communicate our feelings to each other, reading the article for the first time made me feel more connected to my father than I had in a long time.

Newspaper article.

---

8   Dan Devine, "Romano Embodies Riverview Tradition," *Sarasota Herald-Tribune*, 1994.

The momentum continued. During my senior year, I received some All-State team recognition and recruitment letters increased. They were followed by phone calls. I started thinking that college football might be my ticket to getting to college and earning a degree. My challenge was that I had no clue how the recruitment process worked, much less the rules of engagement when conversations began. I relied heavily on others, all the while remaining confused and feeling inadequate. Even so, I received my first official invitation to visit the University of Pennsylvania, the Ivy League school in Philadelphia.

My trip was scheduled for January. To say I was nervous is an understatement. Not only was it my first recruitment trip, but it was also the first time I would travel to another state. Plus, I was going north to a much colder environment. It was the first time I heard of "long johns" to keep you warm. I was joined on the recruitment trip by a friend and fellow defensive player on my team. From the moment we landed, I was anxious and excited.

The evening we arrived, a group of us went out to explore the city and campus. What started as a fun night ended poorly for me. Let's just say, a long night out resulted in a longer morning. I was not feeling my best.

That morning, all the recruits piled into vans for a tour of the city followed by lunch at a local favorite for Philly cheesesteak sandwiches. None of that agreed with my stomach. As we pulled into the parking lot of the restaurant, I grabbed my friend's varsity jacket and threw up in it. The rest of the day I tried to hide the jacket and my embarrassed face.

It didn't take long for the stories to spread. By that evening, after I got some color back in my face, there were jokes about the day. I laughed them off, but I had a new sinking feeling in my stomach—this time, from the shame of how I acted. On the flight back home, I stewed about my behavior; I found it hard to believe. I knew better, and my parents had certainly taught me better. Yet in an effort to try to fit in, I was now a self-inflicted outcast. While I apologized to the Penn coaches, I did not have the guidance or wherewithal to follow up with the sincere letters of apology that would have reinforced my true character.

I continued conversations with the University of Pennsylvania coaches. We talked financial aid packages and admission requirements for the school. Despite my attempts to be cautious and guarded, I found myself excited about the prospect of attending the university. I even started thinking about the clothes I would have to buy to stay warm. My parents could sense my enthusiasm and shared in it. Then, one Sunday afternoon, while my family was not at home, I took a call from one of the U. Penn coaches. They said that, unfortunately, things would not work out for me to attend. In desperation, I asked why and pleaded for them to reconsider, but to no avail. It was final: I would not be attending the University of Pennsylvania.

I was devastated. I felt rejected, not good enough. But then it got worse. My sorrow turned into despair. I panicked. Now I had to figure out new plans. *What will I do now? Where will I go to college? Did I blow all my chances?* I quickly had to compose myself and regroup. I still had a path to college—and football, if I wanted it. I just had to think clearly and get my act together. I talked to additional colleges about football and even entertained taking other trips. I was accepted into state universities. At the end of the day, I was fortunate, because I had options. I ultimately chose the one that was right for me. The one that aligned with who I was and where I wanted to go.

To this day, I'm not completely clear on why I did not end up at University of Pennsylvania. Was it my grades or test scores? Were my football skills not good enough? Did they recruit another player better than me? Did my actions on that recruitment trip display character flaws? And the profound question, how would things have been different if I had ended up there?

But before I get too carried away with the "what-if" game, I center myself on the fact that the path I took was best for me and my family, including reasons I could not even grasp at the time (and I will discuss later in the book). And perhaps even more important than the classes I could have taken at the campus were the lessons I learned from the experience. It was the first of many tough situations in my life. But it set me up for how to deal and cope with future ones.

From this experience, I learned that my "why" included higher education. I was passionate about it, and it was too important to me—and to my family—to let it out of my grasp. I realized that you can be at a significant disadvantage when something is new to you. I learned to lean on others to understand the process and how to play the game.

You, too, will face adversity. You can allow it to knock you down, but not keep you there. Adjust accordingly and success is still yours. When you must make a tough decision about your future, rely on how you've prepared yourself to get there.

While I never received a degree from the University of Pennsylvania, it still taught me a lot—things I would have never learned in one of their classrooms. If I had ended up there, I don't think I would have written this book, much less this chapter. Plus, I never had to worry about buying long johns!

Some of the students I meet have the false impression that their career will skyrocket if they do all the right things—or vice versa, that they'll never have a chance to lift off if they make a mistake. That's not how it works. If they do the right things, they will experience success. But it's inevitable that they will also face challenges and hardships. And when they face adversity, they're better off believing it's a temporary detour on their unique path.

Maybe the best way for you to think of your camino is more like a roller coaster . . . so hold on and enjoy the ups and downs, top speeds, and loops along the way . . . and the occasional getting sick in your friend's jacket.

CHAPTER 7

EDUCATION CHANGES LIVES

remember the first time I stepped foot on a university campus alongside my mom, dad, and brother. It was a family trip to get me settled into my dorm as I started my freshman year. After we set up my room, we walked the grounds.

I'd already toured the university. But it felt different seeing it with my family. We were in awe of the size of the buildings and the number of students. The energy and buzz were exciting, but it was more than that. It was as if there was a collective sense of accomplishment as we walked together. It kind of felt like we had made it. As a family, we had put such an emphasis on education. College was *our* dream. Now, finally, we were here. We were taking the first steps in changing our family's trajectory. It was a big deal for all of us.

Apparently, we're not the only ones who feel that way. Time after time, the students hear the importance of higher education from our speakers. Whether it's a university, college, technical school, education program, or any other postsecondary option, life-changing opportunities present themselves with each degree or certificate.

Education is the great equalizer in life. Studies show that you can improve your chances for higher pay, homeownership, and health outcomes as your education level increases. It's not a coincidence; it's a direct correlation. But our parents and grandparents didn't depend on the statistics to know that. They understood that better than anyone. That's why they made the sacrifices they did.

Your first step on a higher education campus, while critical, is not the most important. More indicative of your success is how you step off the campus. In order to reap the full benefits of an education, speakers ask students to **make the investment, learn how to learn,** and appreciate that their education **impacts others**.

Make the Investment

Whenever the topic of college or another higher education institution comes up with our speakers, the costs associated with it are one of the first factors discussed. It's clear, rightfully so, that students are concerned with the tuition required to pursue higher education. It's expensive, even scary how much it costs to go to college. That's why our speakers implore the students not to think of it as a cost or a burden. Rather, they encourage them to plan on it as an investment.

If you think of it as an investment, you'll expect and realize a high rate of return on your investment. Data shows that higher education equals higher pay. Without an education, you limit your earnings potential. Without an education, you realize an opportunity cost. What could have made you money ultimately loses you money. All a result of inaction driven by the fear of investing in yourself.

The students seem to become calmer about the cost when they learn of financial assistance programs. Over the years, funding and lending options have increased and become more available for students looking to cover their higher education costs. Financial aid from the government, foundation grants, nonprofit scholarships, and philanthropists have provided students with more access to the money they require to purse their education. Those same entities provide students with additional resources so they can fully understand each option and plan their financial stability. Students and parents do not have to do this on their own.

The students are left thinking, *If others are willing to invest in me, shouldn't I bet on myself as well?*

The value of an education has lasting power. You can't lose it. If you face financial hardship, banks and creditors can take away your cars, house, and material things, but they can't collect on your degree. That's your ticket to re-create wealth. And another intangible, yet very influential, result of an education is the credibility factor. Many of our speakers are convinced that the degrees next to their name give others confidence and trust in their abilities.

The case is clear. Higher education pays dividends. But speakers are sympathetic to the high-cost barrier. Their point is that it's worth it, and there are many ways to make the financial commitment doable. I agree, because I know from experience.

I lived through it when I went to college. I'm not sure who was more concerned with costs of college . . . my parents or me. Not only was it the classes, but also the books. Then there were dorms or apartments for rent. And of course, I had to eat. Then, if I wanted to visit home, I had to come up with gas money.

These are financial constraints that many college students face, regardless of their family or financial background. While it can be stressful, it's also manageable. You learn to navigate and to be resourceful.

At the same time, there are ways you can supplement funds and cut your costs while you're in college. For money, I applied to countless scholarships and spent many hours filling out financial aid forms. I also worked internships and jobs for pay. To mitigate my costs, I found ways to be creative with my diet, like sneaking food to my dorm from the cafeteria. You'd also be amazed at how many different meals you can make with mac 'n' cheese. As president of my fraternity, I lived and ate for free. (However, the stress that came with that role probably outweighed the cost savings.)

If you speak to most college students, you'll hear some

humbling and funny stories of how they managed to afford college. They will also tell you that the creativity, discipline, and fortitude they exemplified to make it work financially helped them grow as much as sitting in the classroom. Attending college is not just about the degree. It's also about the experiences and people you encounter while you're there.

And if you think receiving the diploma at your graduation is rewarding, just wait until you pay off your student loans. For me, that was a big milestone to celebrate. One of the three proudest checks I've ever written was helping my mom purchase her house. A second was paying off my student loan. (In case you're wondering, buying my wife's engagement ring was the third.)

The pride, growth, and benefits you earn from higher education pay off over your lifetime. If you were to conduct a valuation of a college degree, you'll find that not only is it worth the investment, but it's actually worth every penny.

Learn How to Learn

No, it's not a mistake or typo. There's intention behind the phrase *learn how to learn*. Many of our speakers have realized that when they arrived at college, they weren't prepared. They weren't equipped with the fundamental skills enabling them to study and succeed in college. Even those who graduated at the top of their class in high school fell behind in the college classroom setting. High school may have been easy, but college was not. They had to rethink and readjust their learning habits. If not, they risked failing or having to drop out. It was a real wake-up call.

If our speakers could go back in time, they often share they would take their high school learning more seriously. They would take advantage of the tools and resources offered. They would listen to their teachers more carefully. They would build the learning skills and foundation that would serve them in college.

One of our speakers learned this lesson even before college. RC was a model high school student. But that wasn't always the case. He had a big scare leading into high school that kept him in line for the rest of his school days. In middle school, RC found ways to save time and cut corners. On one occasion, he cheated on his homework. Then the teacher caught him. He was mortified and embarrassed.

Considering the emphasis his parents and grandparents put on academics, he couldn't bear the thought of his actions jeopardizing his chances for higher education. From that point on, he never took the easy way out. He controlled his own destiny at that point because he made school and grades his top priority. It paid off when he was accepted into Stanford University.

Regardless of when they had their epiphany, many of our speakers admit that they reached a moment when they needed to make education more of a priority and put in the extra time. Not just enough to get by, but the additional effort so they could excel. Just as they treated their commitments to sports or recreational activities, education is much the same. It requires focus, practice, and time to improve.

When students ask how they can learn to learn, speakers provide a long list of things for them to consider. They encourage them to institute study habits—a concept that was foreign to our speakers before college. Listening to lectures, taking notes, and understanding theories is not intuitive. Everyone learns and studies differently.

So take the time in high school to identify what works best for you. Studying in groups can be helpful and motivating. Yet it shouldn't be the only way you study. Give yourself personal space to think and learn. Manage and maximize the time you spend on learning by identifying the right blocks of time in which you can stay focused. Finding the right setting is key. You'll quickly recognize if a spot is too distracting. Some study best in the morning, some in the evening. No amount of caffeine or sugar is a substitute for rest.

I see the students jotting down in their notebooks all the helpful learning nuggets. But the thing our speakers wish they would have done more of and suggest with urgency is reading. They tell the students to READ, READ, READ. If there's one thing they all say they would have done differently, it's read more. The need for and the power of reading skills became abundantly clear to them on day one of college classes. It doesn't matter the course, teacher, or degree. Reading is a must. It can make or break your college career.

Some of our speakers admit they weren't big readers growing up. Their excuse was that they didn't like to read. But their real reason is that they felt they weren't good at it. It was hard for them. They struggled with it at an early age. The difficulties for them associated with reading took the fun and joy out of turning pages in books.

Perhaps reading was not something they regularly saw at home. Rather than books and reading becoming a fixture in their settings, they were anomalies—just a requirement for school and homework, but not something done in your free time. Ask our speakers now, and they all say they wish they could go back to change this. Learning to read well at a young age can make it fun early on and not a chore later. It can invigorate a passion to learn and think instead of becoming a creative hurdle. It can be an asset in higher education and a career rather than a liability.

As our speakers share this insight, I can't help but nod in agreement. I feel the same way. Growing up, I found reading tough. The language barrier was hard. I didn't like to read. I struggled for a long time. While I eventually caught up with my peers, I still didn't find any joy in it. I only read books if they were an assignment in high school. And like our speakers, I learned the hard way that my reading blind spot and my other study habits, or lack thereof, hurt me. So, like others, I had to work harder to correct or improve my weaknesses. It wasn't easy, but it worked. During that time, I discovered a renewed sense of interest and excitement for reading. Unexpectedly, I had come to appreciate the knowledge, pleasure, and fun that comes with reading.

I guess better late than never. But like our speakers, I wish I could go back in time and change my reading habits. While I may not be able to transport myself, I do have a fresh start with my kids. Reading is something we focus on. My wife and I try to read every night with our kids. Sometimes they're more excited about it than others, especially my daughter—a feeling I could relate to at that age.

I tell her about my experiences with reading. I explain how important reading is and how several members of our family continue to struggle with reading. Those who have had challenges wish they would have put more time and energy into it because without the skills to read, they feel behind and limited. I tell her I don't want her to feel the way I did in the classroom when we took turns reading aloud, or the way I felt around my friends when they talked about their favorite books. Rather, I want her to feel proud of the time and effort she puts into reading.

My commitment to my daughter, my family, her teachers, and myself is to help her read—to demonstrate its importance, empower her to learn, and teach her to grow.

While we're proud of our family history, one thing we don't want to do is repeat our struggles with reading and writing. My daughter is part of rewriting that for the future.

Nightly reading time with my daughter.

Impacts Others

The discussions about education and college spur many questions from the students. As the speakers answer their questions, I can see looks of surprise, shock, and stress on the students' faces. The enormity of the importance and influence of an education hits them hard. Even if they've heard the same things from their parents or teachers, it's another thing coming from the speakers. It's as if they need to hear it from someone else, someone who isn't too close to them but is credible and can speak with candor and experience.

That's exactly what they got when Teresa told her story of how she realized the importance of an education. Teresa came from a single-mother family. As she puts it, her family didn't have much money growing up. But that didn't prevent Teresa from wanting all the toys and clothes that others around her had. When she pestered her mother about buying her something or complained she didn't have the newest things, her mother would humbly reply, "*Mija*, if you want more, then get an education." It was a statement she heard often, but it didn't resonate early on.

Teresa was not necessarily on the college track when she was in middle school and early high school. She grew up in a neighborhood where no one had aspirations for college. She hung out with a group with a high propensity to get into trouble. Fortunately, she had a physics teacher who saw potential in Teresa and gave her hope and direction. She had her turning point when she realized college was possible for her.

Teresa went on to receive her bachelor's, master's, and doctorate degrees. Along the way, she realized the joy, pride, and fulfillment her accomplishments brought her family. Her journey continued as she dedicated her work to assist other students and families in reaching their full potential. She's not only seen how her education has changed her life, but also how it impacts others. She's witnessed firsthand countless times the residual effect that education brings an individual, family, and community.

Guest speaker Teresa.

The students listen and take it to heart when our speakers suggest: *This is not all about you. You're not just doing it for yourselves. Whether you know it or not, accept it or not, this is about others as well.*

While our speakers may have been the ones physically headed to college, there were others closely watching and living vicariously through them. For grandparents and parents, it was the closest thing they would have to an education. Younger siblings and cousins observed intently to understand the way it worked. The college experience is stressful enough. To know you have others watching your moves and depending on your success adds even more pressure. That worrying may peak when you get to college, but it builds for years before.

The discussion of college is different across families. Some parents support the dream of an education. Some don't and pass it off as a fairy tale. Some say they do, but change their mind when decisions have to be made. Some don't know enough to know what to think or do. The expectations of parents may vary as well. They expect you to go, or they forbid you to attend. For those with supportive families, the task is a little easier and more enjoyable. For those with skeptical families, the work is lonelier. Either way, students have something to prove to their families. If a student succeeds, they change their own path, as well as their family's path. Even the most resistant of families cannot deny that.

One of the videos I played for the students captured the power and potential of education at its best. It included remarks by Jaime Casap, the former Chief Education Evangelist at Google. A first-generation American, Casap personally knows the power of education. He attended high school, college, and graduate school, then saw his path change his family's destiny, all in just one generation. He paints the picture of the potential that education can have not only on one individual, but also on their family and community.[9]

---

9 "Saving the Silver Bullet: Jaime Casap at Tedx Fargo," September 1, 2013, https://www.youtube.com/watch?v=FbXgCLMl9R4.

Regardless whether you see education as an opportunity, burden, sacrifice, responsibility, privilege, or duty, you can't deny that it creates change. Not everyone gets a shot at it. If you do get the chance, be mindful that others are watching what you do with it. Be aware that your choices will not only change your life, but also will impact those around you.

Mi Camino

No one in my family attended college. No one knew what it took to get there. But that didn't matter. They were convinced that if I could get there, it would change the trajectory of our family. They fully believed and subscribed to the theory that education could change lives.

They did all they could to have me see it that way too. Poppy and Pepe wanted me to have a job where I could use my mind, not physically exhaust my body like them. When I worked at the restaurant with Poppy on weekends and holidays, he would come up to me during the busiest moments and say, "See, you think it's easy?" It was his coarse way of making a point that an education gives you options for your career. In his mind, I had a chance to choose my career, not my career choosing me.

I didn't require much convincing. I wanted to go to college. I wanted to pursue opportunities that required a college degree and experience. When I went to college and started classes, I think we all figured I was on my way. Continue the hard work and studying, and a job would be waiting for me. All I had to do was graduate. Just as I was nearing the finish line to graduate, everything changed. The dream became a nightmare.

My senior year in college, Poppy's cancer got bad. Bad turned into worse. Then he died. The emotional distress was tough enough, but there was so much else to figure out. The restaurant and our family finances were in disarray. I had to be there to take care of my mom and brother.

At first, I tried to juggle school and being back home, making the nearly five-hour trip back and forth to attend classes while also making family arrangements. But it became too much. I was on the verge of potentially failing my classes, so I withdrew for the semester. The painful part was having to submit Poppy's death certificate as proof of my reason. The man who wanted me to graduate from college the most was the reason I had to leave it.

I was planning to come back the next semester. Then I realized my family's recovery could take longer. I thought maybe a year. Finally, I conceded and figured I should make plans to be home indefinitely. I had to forget about college so I could take over the family business.

But my mom would have nothing to do with that plan. She pushed back. She said that she and Poppy didn't make all the sacrifices for me to go to college and then drop out, regardless of the circumstances. She made me go back the next semester. She promised me she would manage. She was not hearing my case or accepting my plans. I was going back to graduate. That was that.

I almost lost the chance to change my life with an education. I nearly did not return to campus to finish what I started.

If I hadn't finished college, maybe my brother wouldn't have gone. Statistics suggest my children wouldn't go. The promise of generational change was almost lost. To this day, I make sure I never forget the opportunity I had to start AND finish higher education.

My dad's father never stepped foot on a college campus. My dad didn't until he was close to 50. I was 18 years old when I stepped foot on a college campus. My son and daughter were less than one year old. In my path, I learned it's not just about stepping on campus; it's about how you step off as well. To fully realize how education can change your life, you have to finish what you started.

CHAPTER 8

SEIZE OPPORTUNITIES

My childhood soccer coach always told my team to "look up" for the opportunity on the field. Play smart and build your game with short passes, he said. But always be prepared for an opening to make the deep pass that leads to a goal and the win.

He invested so much time in us that he wanted us to "look up" not only as players, but also as young people looking for their future off the field. He presented us each a plaque with a set of core principles to live by on and off the field:

- R (Respect, Recognize, Remember)

- C (Commitment, Courtesy, Confidence)

- M (More, Manners, Moderation)

- P (Prepare, Potential, Plan)

The Championship Years
with
Coach Ed

☆1985 Goalbusters	10-1-0	1st Place SUSL
☆1986 Goalbusters	9-0-1	1st Place SUSL
		City Cup Champs
☆1987 Goalbusters	11-1-0	1st Place SUSL
		City Cup Champs
		Inter-League District Champs
☆1988 Sarasota United	11-5-0	Turkey Bowl Champs
☆1989 Goalbusters	11-0-0	GYSA Division IB Champs
☆1991 Sarasota Strikers	21-1-1	USA GYSA Div I Champs
		Regional C Cup Champs
		State Presidents Cup Champs
☆1992 Riverview JV SoccerRams	14-3-1	JV Tournament Champs
☆1993 Riverview JV SoccerRams	12-4-1	

Respect recognize emember

•*Respect* yourself... don't do anything you may regret or lose sleep over. Respect your teammates... you can not win without their support. Respect your adversary... you never know how much power they may really have.
•*Recognize* the achievements of your fellow teammates. Be humble by always recognizing their achievements first. Your recognition may come later, and it will be that much more important.
•*Remember* those who help you and also those who don't. Over time you can take action accordingly. If you remember, the same mistake should not happen twice.

Commitment ourtesy onfidence

•*Commit* to whatever you do, and do it with 100% of your heart, to the best of your ability and effort. If it is not worth commiting to, then don't bother with the first step.
•*Courtesy* Let the other person make the first move. Don't talk if you don't know. If you can't see, don't go. Courtesy will always be to your advantage.
•*Confidence* is like enthusiasm, it is contagious. When you enter a room, enter with purpose. Be confident that you can do anything that you start out to do.

More anners oderation

•*More* Always do more than you are asked to do. If you are given a goal to achieve, exceed it. Those who exceed expectations are rewarded more than others.
•*Manners* Always keep your temper and be well mannered, no matter what the opposition is doing. An ill-mannered person is already a loser, and compared to a well-mannered person, there is no contest.
•*Moderation* is the key to a healthy and successful life. Moderation keeps you free of the web of excess. Everything should be done in moderation.

Prepare otential lan

•*Prepare* to win, and you will win most of the time... 99% of the game is the preparation.
•*Potential* grows in life just as you grow. Always realize your potential as a person is never completely utilized. There is an endless capacity for potential if you believe in yourself.
•*Plans* should be developed for both the short-term and long-term. Plan short-term goals that are attainable. The short-term plan will be measurable advances to achieve your long-term goal.

I Know You Can Make a Difference...
I Know You Can Do It!

Always Practice R.C.M.P.!
From Coach Ed

Plaque from soccer coach.

I can't help but think of the plaque and Coach Ed during so many of the sessions as our speakers discuss opportunities.

When they discuss opportunities, the word *seize* either prefaces it or soon follows. That's the key action when opportunities present themselves. But there is work to be done before they do. The speakers' advice is that you must **create your opportunities first, information is power**, and **be prepared, then react**.

Create Your Opportunities First

According to our speakers, rarely did the opportunities they seized just happen or pop up out of nowhere. Sure, they all benefited from good fortune or luck. But more times than not, opportunities were created. Speakers put in the time, energy, and plans that produced opportunities. Without creating opportunities first, you have nothing to seize.

Speakers give a lot of insight and perspective on how the students can create opportunities for themselves. The key takeaway is to give themselves the tools they need. Not surprisingly, at the top of the list is an education. Education is the foundation. Opportunities exponentially increase when your education is in place. Ellen Ochoa, the first Hispanic woman to go to space, captured what all our speakers mean with her quote: "I tell students that the opportunities I had were a result of having a good educational background. Education is what allows you to stand out."[10]

---

10   LBA, "I tell students that . . . ," Twitter, April 30, 2021.
https://twitter.com/LBA/status/1388176666858508295.

It's also no surprise to hear the speakers attribute much of their success in creating and seizing opportunities to hard work. It seems that the harder they worked, the more opportunities presented themselves. While education is an equalizer, hard work may very well be the differentiator. Our speakers realized they may not be the most educated or wealthiest in the room, but given the chance, they were confident they would work the hardest. Their hard work is what separated them from the pack.

Perhaps the words of wisdom that are most notable to me are that students should be self-aware. This is important advice for sure. But I'm surprised that it is at the top of the list for our speakers. Their point is that people are constantly watching your actions and taking notice if you are someone they should invest their time in to help or hire. So be mindful of your surroundings, words, moves, and interactions, even when you don't think someone is watching. Things like saying "please", dressing appropriately, and showing your appreciation with a thank-you note may seem simple, but they leave lasting impressions. Demonstrate that you can do them in a genuine way, and folks will remember. People are not only looking to see how you manage yourself in positive settings, but perhaps they are more observant of how you react to adversity or disappointment. That's when true character is displayed, and others will take notice.

One of our speakers who best captured the essence of creating opportunities was Ana. Ana is a first-generation American who defied the odds to graduate from high school (as valedictorian), college, and law school. She's gone on to join one of the biggest technology companies, where she has been increasing her responsibilities and elevating her title ever since. Like most of our speakers, her path is full of heartbreak, challenges, and confusion. Her family is her anchor, and she attributes her meteoric success to her education, hard work, and self-awareness.

Guest speaker Ana.

During college, Ana sought an intern position at the White House. To her astonishment, she was accepted. She found herself in a pool of new interns that included Ivy League students and a Rhodes Scholar. Initially she was intimidated. But she trusted she was there because she herself had created this opportunity. Her mindset, discipline, and work ethic allowed her to flourish in this competitive setting. White House officials took notice and remembered her. Later on, when she graduated law school, she was offered a full-time position. But she had another opportunity to pursue. This time, it was with a technology company.

Students realize that if they listen to some great advice from our speakers, it's not a question of whether they can create opportunities, but how many they can create . . .

Information Is Power

One of the most common phrases our speakers use is, "If only I had known . . ." It's said countless times and reflects how speakers wish they had more information at any given time during their academic and professional careers. If they would have possessed more information, they would have been better equipped to plan and execute on opportunities. A lack of information equals a lack of opportunity. It's another way of saying, "information is power."

Many of our speakers were one of the "firsts" in their family to achieve milestones. First to speak English fluently. First to graduate from high school. First to go to college. First to have a career. These are exemplary challenges and feats for anyone, regardless of whether you're the first in your family to do it. But not having anyone you know experience it before puts you at a disadvantage. Not understanding the rules of the game or the land mines on the field can dictate your triumphs and tribulations.

Our speakers share stories of how they learned the hard way. They conquered some challenges. Others were too much to overcome. They accept the results, but what's most frustrating to them are the problems that could have been avoided or mitigated if they had known more, if they just had more information or understanding before they walked into it.

They don't want the students to go through the same experiences. So they suggest that if the students are willing to read and research, they will build a base of information that can help them react. It won't guarantee a win or prevent a loss, but it sure will improve their odds.

Reading gives you instant access to information. Speakers suggest that students should read anything they can get their hands on, and I agree. Read about things that interest you and things that don't. Reading expands your knowledge base and creative problem-solving skills. If you read about a college, career, or role model that interests you, then research it. Research is a deeper dive into learning about what sparks your interest. The information you're looking for is literally at your fingertips. All you have to do is type in the subject on a computer or phone or visit a library. It's accessible and empowering.

But as intuitive and easy as technology makes it, don't underestimate the things you can learn from talking with people. You'll learn things you won't find online. The personal connections go a long way.

Once you read and research, you have to react. Now that you have the information, do something with it. You've done the work, so you might as well put it to use. Let it feed a plan.

One speaker took the extra step to illustrate how this all works. Let's say one of the students in the class liked putting things together, such as cars, radios, or appliances. If the student shares that interest with a parent, teacher, or counselor, a career path of engineering may come up. That student can look up the various types of engineering, the qualifications to become an engineer, the colleges that offer that degree, and the requirements to be accepted into those colleges. The student can also ask to meet with engineers to learn about their experiences firsthand. By reading about the topic and researching the profession, the student can create a college and career plan to become an engineer and identify the people who can help them get there.

Information is not only obtained through reading or researching. Often, information comes in the form of real-life experiences as well. Our speakers had to experiment with career ideas before they knew what they wanted or didn't want to do.

Priscilla and John-Michael told it best. Priscilla had so many interests in college that she changed her major three times. After graduating, she went on to law school and landed a job at a law firm. She was set—except that after working at the law firm, she realized she didn't want to be a lawyer. She hit the reset button and started over. This time, she knew what she didn't want to be. She was armed with that self-awareness. She then found herself attracted to work in philanthropy.

Similarly, John-Michael had one idea in mind. He was driven to achieve financial rewards early in his career. No one could blame him, considering his humble roots in his family's restaurant business. But several years out of college and after his first jobs in corporate consulting and in the construction industry, he also changed course. He made the conscious decision that "money" was not his priority. He wanted to pursue something he was passionate about. For him, that turned out to be community engagement.

Priscilla and John-Michael experimented with their careers. They absorbed information through real-life experiences. They went through emotions and feelings they wouldn't necessarily have found in a book or online. Yet these were critical to helping them seize their next opportunities.

Now here's the thing about Priscilla and John-Michael—they're married! They spoke to the students separately, never aware of each other's remarks or comments to the students. But it should be no surprise to them, or those touched by their work, that they are both fine examples of how to seize your opportunities when you learn your passions.

Seizing opportunities is hard. Information will help. Putting in the extra time and energy to investigate and experiment is worth it. In an increasingly competitive landscape for college and jobs, more information can put you a step ahead, while lack of information can cost you.

Be Prepared, Then React

For our speakers, the only thing more frustrating than a lack of opportunity is a missed opportunity. It could be so tough to secure a spot at school, on the team, or in a company, that if they stumbled when an opportunity presented itself, they would stew over it for weeks, if not years. But that didn't happen to them often. All it took was for that to occur once. They recognized that to seize an opportunity, you must be prepared.

How do you prepare? You start with goals. Then you develop the plan (and a backup plan, and a backup backup plan) to reach your goals. Your plan ensures that you're ready when an opportunity presents itself. The moment may come immediately, or sometimes it takes years. But as long as you have a sense of urgency to prepare, you'll be ready. To be clear, being urgent does not mean that you rush it and just go through the motions. Preparation is giving yourself the time and space to think about your future. Not just one year at a time, but with a strategic, long-term focus.

At times, things play out just the way you've planned. But most times, they don't. That's why you have the backup and the backup backup plan. Opportunities and challenges may present themselves when you least expect them. That's why you have to be flexible. Sometimes an opportunity presents itself sooner than anticipated. Other times, a challenge may push back your time frame. Your plan can always be adjusted for unexpected changes. A good plan is reliable and flexible.

The most important part about preparing is not the plan on paper but preparing yourself. Sometimes we can be our biggest obstacle. Self-doubt limits us. Our speakers often found they had to convince themselves that they were worthy of great opportunities. And even then, imposter syndrome could kick in as they questioned if they really belonged or deserved to be in the room with others. This thought process can snowball to the point that doubt paralyzes our willingness to challenge ourselves or take risks. We can become too scared to seize an opportunity. At that point, no plan can help. It's the individual who must turn the page. The good news is that it just takes one small win to get back to your plan.

Advice from Gerardo provided a remedy for this mindset.

As a seasoned professional in government and technology, he attributed his personal growth (and that of others) to confidence. He encouraged the students not to underestimate themselves, but rather believe in themselves. He told them to set the bar high and watch themselves deliver.

Guest speaker Gerardo.

I also appreciated when our speaker Teresa told the students how she approaches seizing opportunities. She said, "When the door opens, walk through it and figure it out later."

She's right. If you give it too much thought, prepared or not, the opportunity can pass you by.

Mi Camino

I've tried to seize my fair share of opportunities. I've also lost my fair share. I've discovered that you don't have to act on every opportunity that presents itself. I learned to explore each of them with diligence but that it's okay to pass on them. I evaluated each opportunity with my mind and heart. I even got out of my comfort zone to pursue unexpected opportunities.

Like our speakers, I believe my experiences are a net positive because I worked hard to put myself in a position to have opportunities, did my homework, and was ready. That's the checklist I manage for every opportunity. And it's the one that led me to the job I'm most passionate about.

As a small business owner in the restaurant business, our family had some good times but mostly tough financial times. When times were hard, my dad had to do the same as any small business owner. He not only cut costs in the business, but he also cut costs at home. One of those costs was our family health insurance. Years later, he was diagnosed with cancer. Despite our inability to pay for health insurance, he received great health care. The doctors, nurses, and staff took care of my dad and his family. It planted a seed in me that if I could ever help someone in the same position, I would.

Fast-forward to when my wife and I moved to Austin. We were introduced to Ascension Seton hospitals. The non-profit hospital system, created more than 120 years ago, has a unique mission to take care of all persons, with special attention to those who are poor and vulnerable. My wife and I initially started as patients. Our children were born at the central hospital. Then, like many parents, we had to take our kids to the children's hospital. We became philanthropically supportive, and I was ultimately asked by the CEO to serve on the healthcare system's Board of Directors. That's where I found out that when you raise your hand with tough questions, you get asked to come lead from the inside. So I left my banking career and joined Ascension Seton as President of the Foundations. Today, my work is dedicated to helping families like mine.

It's an opportunity I unknowingly created, but one I felt comfortable with because I was informed and aware. And it was an unexpected professional detour I could take because I was prepared, even for the unpredictable. Fortunately, I was in a position to seize this opportunity.

I think back to Coach Ed's framed plaque and how much overlap there is with the things speakers say, the way students feel, and how I live my life. The plaque Coach Ed gave me hung in my room for many years. Recently I showed it to my son. I told him the importance of "looking up" on and off the field to seize opportunities. Now that plaque hangs in his room.

CHAPTER 9

CREATE POSITIVE SURROUNDINGS

When I was younger, my parents would always ask me where I was going and with whom. It didn't matter if I was going to the playground with my neighbor or to a movie with a friend. It was always the same questions. I thought it was annoying and unnecessary.

I ask the students if their parents ask them these questions. They sigh and nod with the same irritation I felt toward my parents.

Given some of the testimonies by our speakers, I think the students realize why parents ask those questions. Your surroundings influence your path. Not only what you do with your time, but also where and with whom you spend it can positively impact you or equally undermine you.

Our speakers vouch for the need to create positive surroundings. From their experiences, their paths were brighter and more promising when their surroundings were uplifting. On the flip side, they attribute their darkest moments to an unstable environment around them.

When thinking about creating a positive surrounding, speakers highlight the importance of being mindful of **who you're with and where you go**, knowing that **predictability is reliability**, and **finding balance**.

Who You're With and Where You Go

One constant in our lives is people. We're always surrounded by people. Colorful stories and proven data tell us that the people around you are indicators of your outcome in life. Hang out with positive and encouraging people, and the possibilities for growth increase. Elect to be around questionable and ill-intended individuals, and your chances for honest prosperity diminish.

As our speaker Tomas poignantly told the students, "Who you surround yourself with matters." He should know. For decades, he's been intertwined with the technology and innovation sector. He's seen firsthand how the people you surround yourself with can make your career or break it.

Considering the undisputable evidence, it's critical that you pay attention to those around you. You should be selective about with whom you spend your time. Seek out people who inspire, motivate, encourage, and support you. Befriend those students who are sitting at the front of the class or rais-ing their hands to answer questions. Look to the captain of the debate team, the president of your class, the valedictorian, or the editor of the school paper. These are the leaders in your academic settings you can learn from. If our speakers could create an all-star team, this is the talent pool they would draft. Knowing it would set them up for winning and success.

Surrounding yourself with positive people is not only a good idea as a teenager; it's also a valuable lesson you should practice throughout your lifetime. Our speakers tell the stu-dents that creating a network is one of the most important things they can do. Building a social and professional net-work throughout your lifetime can provide you with endless opportunities and support. If created genuinely, your network should be a group of individuals who collectively invest their time, talent, and treasure to support you. In your teens, that network might be your family, friends, coaches, and teach-ers. In college, it's those you meet in your dorm, apartment, classes, sorority, fraternity, social clubs, campus organizations, or intramural sports. As your career starts and matures, it will be mentors, bosses, and coworkers. Before you know it, the people in your corner will bring others in as well. Your oppor-tunities look better with each introduction. (More on how to "Create a Wide Network" in the next chapter.)

Our speakers realize that they found positive people in positive places. You'll be hard-pressed to find a positive influ-ence in a negative setting. Be aware of your surroundings. It shouldn't take you long to realize if a place attracts those you should be wary of and stay away from. Go to places and venues that foster growth, not deter it. Even if you're with the right people, they may not be able to help you if you're in the wrong place. Bad things can happen to good people in the worst locations. We all know the feeling that something can go wrong when we show up at a questionable place. Don't risk it. Turn around—or even better, don't show up in the first place. It's easier to avoid a bad situation than have to explain it.

Some of our speakers understood the importance and influence of their surroundings. They knew that whom they hung out with and where they hung out could really impact them. So they resisted the wrong crowds and places early on. But some of our speakers didn't see it so clearly. Due to circumstances at home or in their neighborhood, they found themselves with friends with questionable judgment. Their actions may have been harmless and sporadic at first, but the severity and regularity became worse. Even when they consciously knew they must separate themselves from this negative influence, they had a tough time doing it. They felt pulls of loyalty and allegiance to stick by their friends. Sometimes it took the intervention of parents or police to paint the sobering picture that if they did not make a change, they could end up in jail or worse.

Such was the experience of one of our most entertaining speakers, Marc. As an Ivy League graduate and current business owner, Marc has one of the most extensive networks of friends and contacts in our community. This is a far stretch from when he was growing up. As a youngster, he found himself hanging out with a group of four boys who did everything together—especially get into trouble. Marc started seeing the writing on the wall. He had to pull away from this band of friends, and he had to deal with his feelings of disloyalty and betrayal.

When Marc shared the story with the class, one of the students asked what happened to the other three friends. He replied that one was in jail, one was dead, and no one knew where the other one was. While it may have been a hard call for Marc to change the "with" and "where" in his life, we can all agree it was the right one.

Regardless of when you come to the conclusion, there's no doubt that people and places influence your future. Our speakers point out that the sooner you realize that whom you're with and where you go matter, the better off you'll be. Just don't wait until it's too late.

Predictability Is Reliability

Some of our speakers' lives were marred with uncertainties. They didn't know where they would eat dinner, shower, or sleep some nights. The inconsistency in their lives caused turmoil and disorder. Sometimes school was the only constant in their lives. It was a place where they could learn, but it also gave them solace in a consistent routine. So it's no surprise that whenever they could, they tried to find a predictable schedule, one that took away the uncertainty and fears of the day and replaced them with reliability. That made them feel safe. And any worthwhile path should feel safe.

No speaker desired that stability in their lives more than Rich. Growing up with split parents, he faced constant disruption at home. At one point, his mom and her boyfriend moved Rich and his brother to California with promises of a better life. Unfortunately, it didn't pan out that way. They found themselves living out of their van, with no home base to eat, sleep, or wash. Rich would have to sneak into the dormitories at The University of California, Los Angeles (UCLA), campus to take showers.

He didn't like the instability in his life. He craved more certainty. He wanted a home, and he wanted security. It motivated him to make that life for himself. He left Los Angeles and went on to college and law school, then rose to the top of his law firm and became a partner. A legal case brought Rich back to Los Angeles to take depositions. While there, he purposely made a separate excursion to UCLA to visit and reflect. This time, as he walked the campus, he wasn't trying to sneak around to find a shower. He wasn't panicked or distressed. Now he was secure, and his life and career were stable. His life had come full circle. He changed his path from uncertainties and instability to predictability and reliability.

Predictability is a common pillar throughout the lives of our speakers. Today, it's part of their success. When the students ask the speakers what a day in their life looks like, they're surprised to hear how structured the speakers' days are. They have set times to wake up (usually before 6:00 a.m.), exercise, eat, work, and even have fun.

They scheduled nearly every hour of the day, even blocking

their calendar for free time. When the students ask why they schedule everything, the speakers explain that it gives them the structure they need to be successful. It provides the daily road map to be productive. If they are disciplined and follow it, they know there's a sense of accomplishment at the end of the day.

This demonstrates the importance of a routine. If you know what's happening that day, week, or year, you can plan your path and future accordingly. Sure, things can change. But the reliability of known and trusted people and places in your day can significantly improve your chances of succeeding.

Sticking to a predictable and reliable routine has been a hallmark for our speakers throughout their lives. Our speakers filled their schedules with sports, music lessons, church, and community service—not only because of their interest and passion in the activities, but also because with those commitments, they (and their parents) knew where they would be. Equally important, this meant they couldn't be somewhere else, such as in a more questionable setting. It also provided results. Grades improved, social stress was reduced, and they found themselves better equipped to manage the unexpected.

They also found that the more they created an environment that was predictable and conveyed reliability, others wanted to be part of it. Others took note of the results and wanted to join them. That extended to others. This becomes contagious and multiplies. As a result, they not only helped themselves; they also helped others.

All the talk about routine and schedule is music to my ears. Like most of our speakers, growing up I required an order of events to thrive. Without it, I was lost. My focus drifted, and I became prone to making poor decisions. My schoolwork suffered, and my commitments faltered. I learned that I was better when I was sharp and on schedule. For me, that meant a daily routine of school, practice, dinner, and homework. On the weekends, I worked. I may not have liked it every night, but I knew it was what I needed if I wanted to reach my potential.

The students question the fun in this approach. We have to remind them that none of the speakers say they never had fun. In fact, it's a lot easier to laugh and smile when you're doing all the right things to ensure a predictable and reliable future.

Finding Balance

As they listen to each speaker, the students go through a roller coaster of emotions. One story has them laughing. Just minutes later, a shared vulnerable moment has them in tears. The swings from joy to sadness are emotionally exhausting. If it's taxing for the students to hear it, imagine how draining it is for the speakers to live it. How did they cope with it? They found balance.

For every high, there's a low. For every win, there will be a loss. For every good day, there's a bad one that follows. This isn't just the case for our speakers. This is life. To get through the extremes, our speakers cherish and celebrate the wins, while appreciating and learning from the losses. But you don't want the wins to give you a false comfort level or the losses to deter your drive. You have to have a balanced frame of mind, recognizing and appreciating the lessons that come with each experience and result.

That can be a taxing proposition. The emotional and mental toll can be enough to take you off your course. That's why our speakers encourage the students to take care of themselves. Your body, mind, and soul require to be in a good place in order for you to meet your true potential. Find the interests and hobbies that heal you and give you peace of mind. Take a break from the grind to appreciate the journey. Pause to reflect and rejoice in your moments.

The advice I like most that the speakers give is to treat yourself. It's some of the best advice my Poppy gave me. Not only did he say it, but he also put money behind it.

My freshman year of college, my family drove me to my dorm to get settled and wish me luck. After hours of my mom cleaning (more like bleaching) my room, organizing my clothes, and stashing food in my closet, we went out to dinner. It was an Italian restaurant. It probably wasn't on the list of the finest restaurants in town, but it was one of the best meals I've ever had. I don't remember a restaurant experience where I enjoyed being with my family more. We laughed, told stories, even shed a few tears of joy. It's what we all needed, as the next day we would be saying goodbye as they headed back home.

The next morning, they came to the dorm for one final goodbye. In an unexpected gesture, Poppy reached for his pocket and money clip. He pulled out his credit card. My father never used a credit card. He was a cash-only guy. In fact, I didn't even know he had a credit card. He then handed me the credit card and leaned in to say that he knew I'd have tough times at college. I would be stressed. I might even cry. But on those days, he said, go to the Italian restaurant and treat yourself to a good meal. He told me to remember my family and let them buy me dinner.

That invitation meant the world to me. I never took him up on it. But I didn't have to. That gesture gave me the balance I needed.

Mi Camino

I didn't realize how important my surroundings, especially the people, are until it mattered most. When Poppy passed away, my mom, Jose, and I couldn't have gotten through it without the support of the people in our lives. I think the three of us are strong and resilient. But the weight of the emotional, financial, and mental distress from Poppy's death would have broken us if not for the love and care extended to our family.

The assistance was boundless. Financially, friends held fundraisers and personally loaned or donated money to cover medical bills. They created accounts to cover college expenses. They made funeral arrangements and coordinated meals.

The help continued for years, and support still exists today. This support system has ensured predictability in our lives by being a constant presence. Just like when Poppy was alive, they've joined us in our milestone celebrations. They were at my college graduation and attended my wedding. They balanced mourning our loss with memories of happiness through videos, pictures, and stories of Poppy. They helped Mom with selling the restaurant, finding jobs, and, most importantly, coping with her grief. They were the role models Jose and I needed to see and strive to be.

Everyone who helped or assisted had been touched by Poppy. He spent years creating positive surroundings, not just for himself, but also for his family, friends, employees, and customers. That network of support has continued well beyond his passing, touching and benefitting the paths of many.

The next time a student's parent asks them where they are going and with whom, I hope they won't give their parents grief about the question, but rather pay more attention to their answer.

CHAPTER 10

ASK FOR HELP

I come from a family where we—especially the men—did not ask for help. It's not that we didn't need it. I think everyone in my family can point to times and instances in their lives where an extra hand or guided assistance would have helped tremendously. Perhaps my family was too proud to ask for help. Or perhaps they just didn't know what kind of help existed or know how to ask.

I realized that if I wanted to finish high school, go to college, find a job, and even help my family after my father's death, I couldn't be like my family. I needed to ask for help.

Over the last several years during Camino Forward, I've recognized that I'm not the only one who comes from a family whose grandparents and parents were too proud to ask for help or unaware of how to ask. However, new surroundings, higher expectations, and available resources have led their children and grandchildren to ask for and receive help.

Our speakers similarly had needs that prompted them to ask for help. Through their experiences, they found that when asking for help, you should **start early, create a wide network,** and **think about who's helping you.**

Start Early

The students often ask the speakers if they've had any regrets in their lives. Most speakers reposition the question to not call out specific regrets, but rather tell students things they would have done differently.

One thing many of the speakers say they would have done differently is to ask for help early. They implore the students not to wait to ask for help until it's too late. Our speakers wish they would have asked for help earlier in their academic and professional careers. They're left wondering if their grades would have been better if they had approached their algebra teacher at the beginning of their school year with questions. They wonder if their college options might have expanded if they'd had a conversation with their high school guidance counselor their freshman year rather than at the end of their senior year. They wonder whether they would have received a promotion if they'd nurtured a relationship with their boss when they started their job.

The common takeaway is that your chances for success

improve when you ask for help early on, so the advice or help you receive may impact you over a longer period of time. If you wait too long, you may be left wondering, "What if I had approached them sooner?"

We also hear of examples of speakers who didn't have to go through the steps of proactively seeking help. At times, wisdom and guidance were offered unexpectedly by others. Their responsibility was to recognize when an early genuine hand was being extended to lift them up. That hand might not always be there. Not grabbing it when it's offered may mean losing out on an opportunity to grow.

The early and extra effort that one person invests in a student can be the catalyst that launches that student's path for positive change. It is especially impactful when a student has the deck stacked against them based on where they come from. Students who face inherited challenges can feel as if they're starting the race without a chance to win. In many ways, their starting point is well behind the starting line. If they can't make up that ground early, they may never catch up to the leaders. Some may even drop out of the race. It's parents, friends, teachers, and coaches who can not only help them make up that ground early but also give them the boost they require to lead the pack.

I thought I was out of the race when I was young. By the time I finished second grade, I was behind my classmates in reading, writing, and speaking. My confidence was low. I wasn't motivated. Rather, I felt ashamed and had no drive to make myself better. At that age, I'm not sure I knew what help looked like, much less know how to ask for it.

Fortunately for me, that all changed when I started the third grade and walked into Mrs. Goolsby's class. I'm not going to lie, the first day I walked into her classroom and met her, I was flat-out scared. You didn't have to be around her long to realize that Mrs. Goolsby was serious, stern, and didn't put up with a bad attitude. She had seen it all through her years of experience. She was tough. But more importantly, she was fair, and she cared. I don't think it took Mrs. Goolsby long to figure me out. I wasn't asking for it, but it was clear to her that I needed help . . . immediately, before I completely lost my path.

Mrs. Goolsby's expectations were the same for all her students—high. I was no exception. But she realized that I needed additional support to meet them. She spent extra time with me. She challenged me. She believed in me. And it worked. By the end of the year, I was receiving straight As. I was raising a confident hand in class to answer questions. I read aloud with pride. My self-esteem skyrocketed.

Mrs. Goolsby single-handedly impacted my life. She put me on a trajectory to excel in school, all because she not only knew I needed help, but she also understood I needed help early. If she didn't provide the extra help I needed, I might never have received it. Before her, I was a below-average student who couldn't read or write English well and almost was held back in the first grade. She turned my insecurity into confidence. She transformed my complacency into motivation. She freed me from fear and pushed me to succeed.

I may not have known how to ask for help in the third

grade, but I'm thankful I could recognize that I needed it and see when it was being offered.

Every year when Tomas and Ellie start a new school year, I think of Mrs. Goolsby. I hope they'll have a teacher who's as positively impactful on them. I'm not necessarily expecting their teachers to teach like Mrs. Goolsby, but I sure do hope they offer the same help Mrs. Goolsby offered me early on and that my kids accept it.

Create a Wide Network

Our speakers always attribute their accomplishments to the help they received from others. The more people helped them, the greater their success. So, the takeaway is simple for the students: If you want to be successful, you must create a wide network of supporters.

Creating a social, academic, and professional network of contacts is critical to identify, pursue, and secure opportunities. As our speakers often suggest, it truly can come down to who you know. The more time you spend building your network, the greater your chances of success.

Many speakers connect their ability to navigate the academic and professional landscape to having good mentors. After seeing some of the looks on the students' faces when the topic of mentors comes up, I've realized that it's a novel concept for many of them. So, we spend some time talking about what a mentor is. A mentor relationship can take several forms. At the core, it's someone you can learn from. The term *mentor* is also synonymous with *role model, sponsor, friend, confidant*, and *advocate*. Regardless of what you call it, what they do is simple: They help.

When it came to asking for help, our speakers looked to everyone, everywhere. They started their network with their inner circle of support, then extended outside of it. They didn't just confine themselves to familiar faces; they also extended their reach to those with different experiences from them or to those they might not even know. They had to proactively seek an introduction, then build a relationship with them. They found that by casting a wide net, the help they received was often unexpected and more impactful.

Creating a wide network takes time. And it shouldn't be viewed as a one-and-done kind of project. Your support system should grow along with your personal and professional interests and endeavors. Your network will continue to evolve throughout your life. Sure, it can be rewarding for your career. But more importantly, it should be fun and an endless way to get to know people.

Once you've created your network, don't be afraid to use it. Sometimes folks in your network will offer to help. But if they don't, you have to be willing to ask. Asking for help makes some of us uncomfortable. One trick our speakers suggest is to look at it as though you're asking for advice. Frame the conversation as information gathering as you explore options in school or work.

One national figure who framed this concept well is Christy Haubegger, founder of *Latina* magazine. I regularly pulled up her quotes for the students, including this one:

I find myself making an amalgamation of role models. I take a little bit from here and a little bit from there. They're not all Latino and they're not all women. Some of my most wonderful mentors have been completely unlike me. Anglo men, for example, who, for one reason or another, think that who I am or what I'm doing is interesting and worthwhile. If you sit around and say, "I'm waiting for someone who looks just exactly like me to reach in and give me a hand," you won't get it. It will take forever. You have to look for your role models as you go along, wherever you can find them.[11]

Her perspective highlights the importance of not only seeking advice and help, but also the value that comes from getting that support from a wide network.

I also like how Haubegger puts it in a more direct way: "Take help where you can get it."

I wonder if she's free to be my mentor . . .

Think about Who's Helping You

During one of our sessions, when we discussed networking and utilizing your relationships, one of the students brought up a very poignant point. He inquired about the difference between "utilizing" and "using." His view was that it felt

---

11   Rose Castillo Guilbault and Louis E.V. Nevaer, *The Latina's Guide to Success in the Workplace* (Santa Barbara, CA: Praeger, 2012), p. 80.

disingenuous or even fake to ask people for help when it was just benefitting you.

It's a fair observation. If not done the right way, building a network and reaching out to people for help can come across as self-serving and self-promoting. That's why our speakers spend time telling the students that they should always think about those who are helping them.

Building a network, requesting an introduction, or asking for help does not have to feel selfish. It can be done in an authentic and humbling way in which your interaction with individuals is respectful and genuine. You can simultaneously fulfill their personal passions and objectives to create a mutually inspiring and beneficial relationship that serves both of you.

Most importantly, you should think of your engagement with anyone as a relationship, not a transaction. A transaction is a one-off interaction with no basis of connection. There is no trust, appreciation, or respect in a transactional exchange. It's simple currency with no long-term potential. Rather, a relationship is a mutually engaging interaction between individuals. A relationship is a two-way street with both parties invested in the well-being and success of each other.

Perhaps the most important rule as you build a relationship with a mentor-like figure is to be respectful of their time. In fact, time is one of the most appreciated and valuable things a person can offer. That means you should be sensitive to the person's time and considerate of how, when, and where you reach out to them. Timing is everything. Realize that they have personal and professional commitments and so may not always be available on your time frame. But when they do take the time to focus on you, make sure you make it easy for them. Show them you realize their time is valuable:

- Meet on their terms (time, location, attire).

- Keep the meetings brief (less than an hour).

- Show up on time when you visit (actually, get there early).

- Do your homework prior to meeting with them and be prepared for your talk (have your story and questions ready to go).

- Go into the conversation with a notepad and take copious notes (after you ask them if you can).

- Leave the meeting with a follow-up or call to action in mind (ask if they can introduce you to someone else).

- Realize that an informal conversation can turn into a job interview (you never know when someone is looking to hire and offer you a job then or in the future).

Our speakers share that the people you approach are more open to help if they know you're serious about asking for help and are mindful of their time.

Our speakers also found that their relationships with mentors and role models were most impactful when they were able to help them in return. Oftentimes, speakers found that didn't take much. Many of these individuals who provide support just want to help you. They value providing a hand up because they received one themselves or wish they would have during their careers. Some mentors learn from you as they gather new perspectives from a different lens. Others can quickly identify a rising star and want to be part of their meteoric ride. They're not asking or looking for anything in return for their support. But a gesture to help and support your mentors or role models in their endeavors will go a long way with them.

There's also a caution when asking for help. Be ready when it's offered. Asking for help is the first step. Listening to and acting on the advice you receive are the next critical steps. When you ask for help, be willing to listen to the advice. You don't always have to act on it or agree with it, but you should at least listen to it. For the advice you receive and agree with, make a commitment to act on it. For the advice you don't follow through on, be prepared to tell that person why you didn't, especially if you're going to ask them for help in the future.

Regardless of the time you spend with a mentor or role model, the rapport you build with them, or the quality of their help, our speakers say it's critical to show your appreciation for those who are willing to help you. According to our speakers, if you're going to ask for help, you need to remember to thank them for their help. That means always saying thank you. All our speakers are fans of handwritten thank-you notes. Sometimes considered a lost art, thank-you notes still represent one of the most dignified and personalized ways to show your appreciation.

But don't stop there. You can show your gratitude in many other ways. Send them an article that reminded you of your conversation, mail a birthday card, make an introduction to another mentor, drop off some cookies, or make a social media post (but check with them first about using their name on such a public forum).

If you're mindful, respectful, and genuine to those who help you, you will undoubtedly shape a long-term relationship with them. Our speakers have relationships with mentors that have extended for decades. They mostly found themselves as the beneficiaries of those relationships. Their mentors helped them get into school, find jobs, and even introduced them to their spouses. But our speakers also contributed to the lives of those who helped them. Sometimes they were aware of their influence immediately. Other times, it was discovered over many years. Regardless, they learned that they did impact them.

I guess that's what happened to me . . .

I clearly benefitted from being in Mrs. Goolsby's class. Every day, I grew and matured. She was invested in me. I often wondered why. Why did she put so much time and energy to ensure a positive path for me? I knew she was a teacher and that was her job, but she went above and beyond.

I think my story and experience had something to offer her. I think I also gave her the opportunity to grow as well. The year I was in her class, Mrs. Goolsby was continuing her education. As part of her training, she asked my parents if I could join her for one of the educational seminars. Together we went and shared our experiences and work together with her colleagues. I remember the pride in her voice when she talked about our relationship. It was clear to everyone that our partnership was mutually positive and impactful. (For me, the best part was when she treated me to my first experience at Burger King afterward.)

One day this past summer, as I was leaving my office and exiting the elevator, I took a quick look at Facebook. The first post I saw stopped me in my tracks. Mrs. Goolsby's son posted that she had passed away. The news devastated me. I had to sit down before I left the building. I thought about her the entire ride home, shed a tear, reached out to my wife and mom to tell them, wrote about it in my journal, and even told my kids about her.

As if the news of her passing wasn't surprising enough, less than twenty-four hours later, her son reached out to me. I had never had any contact with him. But he messaged me to say, "My mother had wonderful thoughts about you when you were in her class." I was floored. For years, I cherished and appreciated the impact Mrs. Goolsby had on my life. What I didn't realize was how much I had touched hers as well.

Mi Camino

As I listen to our speakers share so many great nuggets of advice and wisdom, the one that resonates with me the most is their claim that it's never too late to ask for help. As I hear them share that point, I think of my Tita Chari.

Tita Chari is my mom's youngest sister. Born in Spain, she was a young child when the family moved to Toronto.

She assimilated to her new home and balanced languages and cultures. She became disinterested in school and turned to a career in retail. With time, she married, had two kids, and moved to the suburbs of Toronto. Unfortunately, life took a twist. She divorced and found herself caring for her children and being the primary caretaker of my grandparents, especially Mama during her final years.

Professionally, a run in the property management sector proved to be riddled with challenges. She ultimately found herself without a job. Unemployment turned into financial hardship and led to stress and anxiety. She found herself at a crossroads. With grace and determination, she powered through the challenges to make a new path for herself. She wanted to reinvent herself with a new career in real estate. But she needed help. She would benefit from some professional, financial, and emotional support to give her a chance.

Perhaps due to our family's historic trepidation of asking for help, she was hesitant to reach out for assistance. But as with everything else in my family, there's no chance of keeping a secret. Soon, our family rallied to help her. She made a run at real estate, but the results were not what she expected, so she went back to the drawing board. This time, she started her own company from scratch—a cleaning service for office buildings. This time, she was more receptive to asking for help. She even brought in her son to be part of the business. With time, she has grown her company with a steady business of current and new clients.

I witnessed my aunt's entrepreneurial accomplishments several years ago when I visited Toronto. The circumstances were sad, as I was there for Mama's funeral. The night before the funeral, the family gathered at Tita Chari's for dinner. Late into the evening, she excused herself from the table. She shared that she had to get ready to clean a client's offices (she went at night so as not to disrupt office hours). My cousin was sick and not able to join her that night. The look of exhaustion and fatigue on her face was obvious. Now more than ever, she needed help with her business. This time, she didn't have to ask. My two uncles, another cousin, brother, and I stood up to say we'd go with her to clean the office building. We divided and conquered the job, although I'm not sure she'll be hiring any of us full time considering her high standards.

Even within my own family, I witnessed a cultural change of asking for help. At one point, the patriarchs in my family would have resisted a helping hand. However, I witnessed that mentality change. I saw firsthand how job and health hardships could prompt the strongest of wills to recognize they need help.

It's okay to ask for help. At some point in our lives, we all need help. Help may not always be there when you need it, but you don't know unless you ask.

I can't say I'm the most comfortable person when it comes to asking for help. But I certainly have come to learn of the need and art of asking for help. I'd say I'm now more comfortable offering help. In fact, I don't wait for others to ask me for help; I ask them if I can help them. One can say that's what prompted me to start Camino Forward. My goal was to figure out how to help those who need it, those who don't know they need it, or those who know they need it but can't bring themselves to ask for it.

If you're going to ask for help, you'd better be willing to help others—help goes both ways. That's why our speakers are helping the students. Others helped them, so it's their turn to pay it forward and help others.

AHORA QUÉ? NOW WHAT?

At the beginning of each school year when we kick off our program with a class of students, I stand in front of them full of nerves. This first impression is critical to having them buy into the concept of Camino Forward.

During each session for the remainder of the year, my anxiousness continues. I hope that the theme and speaker of the day will resonate with the students so they continue to be engaged and learn.

By the last session of the year, as we conclude the program, I stand in front of those students with a tremendous amount of pride, gratitude, and appreciation. I know these students have put in the time and energy to learn from others as they plan an academic and professional career that will lead to a brighter future for them and their families.

I started Camino Forward to help solve a challenge I identified in my community. It was a challenge I experienced growing up as well. That is, how do you dream, plan, and implement a future that includes higher education and a career if you don't know what that path looks like? It's hard to find a path you've never seen anyone take it.

Camino Forward exposes students to individuals they can relate to and learn from through a series of speaker forums. Our speakers share their powerful stories and inspiring experiences—including their successes and challenges—to help provide the students with a road map as they think of an academic and professional future.

The conversations, questions, and interactions between our speakers and students led to the development of 8 Themes—represented in this book by eight chapters—that serve as the foundation of the Camino Forward program.

These lessons learned from the stories told, now shared in this book, highlight the following:

- Remember Where You Come From

Remembering where you come from **serves as inspiration** and **shapes who you are,** while motivating you to **help others in your situation**.

- Family Matters

Family molds who we are as we learn from their **adapting to a new normal**, the **limitations** they experienced, the **generational change** they faced, and the **degrees of support** they provided.

- Embrace Your Differences

When you embrace your differences, you understand it's **hard but powerful**, an **advantage, not a disadvantage**, to **share your story**, and to **connect with others with similar differences**.

- Each Path Is Unique

While each one of us has a unique path, everyone should **know your "why," learn from others, adapt and overcome challenges**, and be ready for the **"fork in the road" moments**.

- Education Changes Lives

An education can change your life if you **make the investment, learn how to learn**, and appreciate that your education **impacts others**.

- Seize Opportunities

If you want to seize opportunities, you must **create your opportunities first**, know **information is power**, and **be prepared, then react**.

- Create Positive Surroundings

Your path becomes brighter and more promising when you create positive surroundings by being mindful of **who you're with and where you go**, understanding that **predictability is reliability**, and **finding balance**.

- Ask for Help

When you recognize your need to ask for help, you should **start early, create a wide network**, and **think about who's helping you.**

At the end of each session, I remind the students that our speakers are there to help them. By spending time with them and sharing their most intimate experiences, they are clearly signaling to the students they identify with them, care about them, and want to support them. But our speakers, Camino Forward, family, friends, and community can only do so much for the students. We emphasize to the students that it's incumbent upon them to chart their own path, their own Camino Forward—not just for them, but for their families, friends, and community, now and for the generations to come.

I close this book as I close our sessions . . . My only ask of my students, and now my readers, is that years from now, when my kids and the next generation are sitting in the classroom thinking and planning their future, that the students will come back to share their stories—the good and the bad—so that my kids and our next generation can plan their Camino Forward.

ACKNOWLEDGMENTS

There are so many people to acknowledge and thank for their role in shaping my life, molding my experiences, and making the passion project of Camino Forward possible. I'd like to especially recognize the following:

- The students who inspire this work and show up willing and open to the support of leaders in their community.

- The speakers who shared their stories with vulnerability and humility, especially the speakers who embrace their experiences in the book: Ana, Carlos, Deanna, Erica, Gerardo, Geronimo, John-Michael, Lem, Leticia, Leticia (yes, two of them), Luis, Marc, Maricruz, Miguel (the other Miguel), Priscilla, RC, Rich, Rolando, Teresa, Tomas, Veronica, and Yvette.

- The school administrators, principals, and teachers who took a chance and partnered with someone new with a different idea to help students.

- My madre for having honest conversations about our history and my feelings as I wrote this book.

- My brother, Jose, for championing this idea and reassuring me to share our story with confidence.

- My wife, Katie, for her consistent support, encouragement, and love with this endeavor.

- Ellie and Tomas for thinking it's cool that their Papi is writing a book. (And for choosing the book cover.)

- My family, from Spain to Canada to the U.S., for creating an upbringing filled with love, fun, and respect that fills the pages of this book.

- My friends at various stages of my life who have always extended boundless friendship during the highs and lows.

- The endless number of mentors who have guided my journey.

Camino Forward has been rewarding and motivating while challenging and exhausting at times. But when I think of the individuals who have championed and supported me and this passion project, I'm grateful and ready to tell another story to help someone plan their path.

ABOUT THE AUTHOR

MIGUEL ROMANO, JR. is a first-generation American. He's the first in his family to graduate from high school, college, and graduate school. Throughout his academic and professional experiences, he found himself struggling to dream of, plan for, and execute on his future.

After moving to Austin, Texas, Miguel started a passion project, Camino Forward, which aims to encourage students to develop a career path by drawing inspiration from leaders in their community through a series of speaker forums. The stories shared and lessons learned provide students a road map for their path forward.

Miguel resides in Austin with his wife and two children. He also leads a nonprofit health care foundation and has served in various public and community service roles.